For Sherry

Ken Visiten

I

AM

COYOTE

I

AM

COYOTE

by Geri Vistein

Tilbury House Publishers
12 Starr Street, Thomaston, Maine 04861
800-582-1899 • www.tilburyhouse.com

First hardcover edition: November 2015
ISBN 978-0-88448-466-0
eBook ISBN 978-0-88448-478-3

Library of Congress Cataloging-in-Publication Data

Vistein, Geri.
  I am coyote / by Geri Vistein. -- First hardcover edition.
     pages cm
  Includes bibliographical references.
  ISBN 978-0-88448-466-0 (hardcover) -- ISBN 0-88448-466-1 (hardcover) 1. Coyote--Psychology--Fiction. 2. Coyote--Dispersal--Fiction. 3. Biodiversity--Fiction. I. Title.
  PS3622.I789I25 2015
  813'.6--dc23
                              2015030660

15 16 17 18 19 20 MAP 6 5 4 3 2 1

Interior design by Kathy Squires
Cover design by John Barnett, 4 Eyes Design
Cover photo by Shreve Stockton / The Daily Coyote / www.dailycoyote.net
Printed in the U.S.A. by Maple Press, York, PA

"We move among great powers and mysteries and only glimpse their meanings, the meaning of what it's like to be another creature, and therefore also the meaning of being a self, a person."

—Robert Hass, from *The Poetic Species: A Conversation with Edward O. Wilson and Robert Hass* (Bellevue Literary Press, 2014)

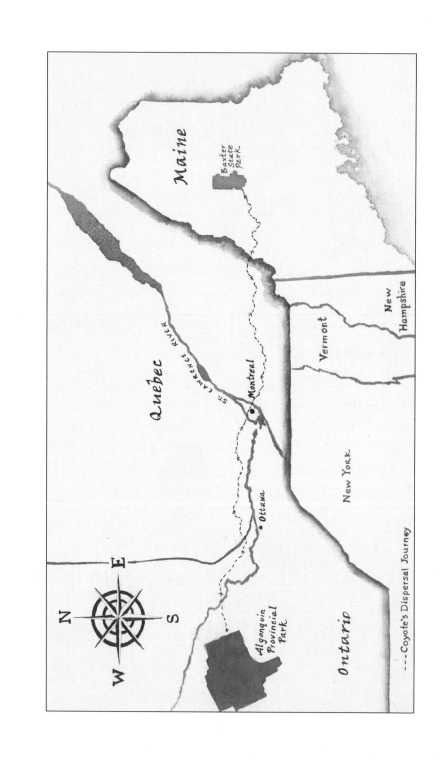

N
W   E
S

Ontario

Algonquin
Provincial
Park

Ottawa

Quebec

ST. LAWRENCE RIVER

Montreal

New York

Vermont

New
Hampshire

Maine

Baxter
State
Park

- - - Coyote's Dispersal Journey

Baxter State Park

The Lookout

The Cabin

Katahdin

- - - - Coyote and her mate journey into Baxter State Park
●●●● Their territory

PROLOGUE

How are we ever to understand and appreciate the intelligent carnivores who live among us so warily and elusively, rarely allowing us even to see them?

As a carnivore biologist, I have asked myself that question many times, and one of the answers that came to me was to write this book. It is about a journey and a life. It is the story of one female coyote, and by extension it is the story of all coyotes on the American continent. It is a story of our humanity as well.

Coyote's journey began in Algonquin Provincial Park in Ontario, Canada, during the late 1960s, when she was a tiny pup developing within her pregnant mother's body. Her journey ended with her death in Baxter State Park, Maine.

She was one of the first coyote pioneers to brave a passage eastward across Canada, traveling unnoticed through Montreal, discovering a way to cross the mighty St. Lawrence River, evading traps and snares, and finally expanding her species' range into Maine. Her journey was one of historic proportions in the return of carnivores to North America's landscapes.

Her journey is not just a metaphor. It is integral to a wide-ranging carnivore's life. The departure of a young coyote from his or her family is no less essential to the survival of the species than the migrations of birds and great whales.

There is the outer journey, but there is also the inner journey in the life of an intelligent, sentient being—and that inner journey is the heart of this narrative. As Coyote journeys through her life—experiencing fear, joy, affection, loss, grief, puzzlement, and acceptance but never anger—I have strived for the words that will render her understandable.

How does one translate the dynamic inner world of these intelligent beings into human terms? I have made every effort to be true to what coyotes are capable of not only in their will to survive but in their experience of life, their relationships with one another, and the emotions we know they experience. Occasionally I have had to reach beyond our present understanding of their inner world, for there is much we don't know. Coyotes possess a unique intelligence and a hidden consciousness of their reality—one that is different from our own but no less vibrant and aware.

Finally, I have interwoven our human history in North America with this intelligent carnivore, attempting to ask—if not to answer—the questions, where have we been and where do we go from here?

I encourage you to trust in the realness of what you are about to read. May this story enrich your understanding of our amazing planet and the incredible beings who share it with us.

1

Late January to Early February 1970

Where she was traveling to, Coyote did not know. Yet somehow the ancient wisdom of her kind would guide her on her journey. In the wintry darkness of this strange place, the light of an iridescent moon led her onward, taking her farther and farther from her forest home. As she trotted along, her thick golden coat sparkled with the recent snowfall that had given way to a clear night sky. The pure white paws on her long golden legs crunched on the cold snow beneath her, each step momentous in her life and the life of her kind.

Twelve darknesses earlier, she had left the sheltering forests of her family's home, traveling eastward. That beautiful, wild place with its pristine lakes and untamed rivers, surrounded by the verdant boreal forests of the north, had been her only home, but the time had come for her to leave her parents and the safety of their care. She had been one of five littermates, with two brothers and two sisters. Now no more than two remained alive. Her surviving brother had left the family and trotted south into the bitter cold and snow twelve moons earlier. She had stayed with her parents, helping them raise another litter of pups when the days turned warm, practicing the skills of a wild hunter and learning how to survive in a world shared with humans—a world that was never safe, never easy. She had learned how to be Coyote.

East, west, north, and south were not concepts she knew or needed to know. The evening sky faded to darkness behind her, and the morning sky lightened ahead of her, but even by night or in storms, she knew where her direction lay. Once out of the protective forests of her family's home, she moved through fields set with snares and steel-jawed traps, fields where guns sent winged messages of death, fields where dogs might give chase not simply for food or to protect a territory, but to kill for the sake of killing.

She traveled relentlessly through the darkness, moving with caution in every step. Her mother had taught her to be wary of easy food lying in her path as if in offering. *Stay away! It is danger!* had been her mother's stern lesson, and Coyote would remember.

In her blood and in the neurons of her cerebral cortex flashed memories of her ancient culture, a culture that had survived millennia of ice, the challenges of living among the giant ones that were no more—saber-toothed tigers, dire wolves, mammoths, and great camels—and the coming of humans to the coyotes' world. Culture, instinct, memory, impulse: Coyote had inherited these from her maternal lineage, and they informed every beat of her heart, every breath taken in and sent out again, every focused thought, every fiber of fur, every look in her eyes, every twitch of her ears. She carried this culture with her, a culture steeped in the will to survive.

Coyote sensed that her journey would be long, for if she was to find a territory of her own, she would need to keep skirting the edges of territories already occupied by wolf or coyote families. She understood the order of her world; her parents had taught her that honoring territorial boundaries was a matter of survival among wild canines. As a pup and adolescent, she had watched her parents repeatedly secure their home by scent marking and howling. Now the territorial boundaries of others led her through narrow, invisible passages and kept her traveling on and on.

As the previous days had passed, her keen nose had sensed a change in the air she breathed. The rich scents of boreal forest, with its fragrant needles waving on primeval trees, its soil pungent with fungi and decaying matter, and its sweet running streams plunging in and out of shadow—she could no longer breathe these familiar scents. They were gone, left behind. In their place her nostrils were filled with the smells of a landscape dominated by humans: fields plowed under by acrid-smelling machinery; human structures and fencing; and the strange, rank odors of domestic animals and their excrement.

Hunger was her constant companion, but she had learned well how to survive the deprivations of winter. Hunger was intrinsic to coyote culture. She pressed on. As each dawn approached, she knew she needed to find a safe refuge in which to rest for the next night's journey. Her acute senses told her that, in this human-dominated landscape, night was her best protector.

Once settled in an obscure hiding place, she would let exhaustion send her quickly into a deep sleep of vivid dreams. Her dreams often called forth her mother's memories and the memories of her ancestors from long ago, memories passed on to her mother's unborn pups as innate genetic consciousness while they grew within her womb. When dreams came to Coyote, that part of her who was her mother and her mother's mother came forth once more.

Coyote's mother also had taken a long journey, but hers had been from the great, wide grasslands of the North American interior, where her ancestors had lived for thousands of years alongside the wolf, grizzly bear, cougar, and Native Peoples. Once, coyote and human cultures had coexisted in harmony and mutual respect, separate nations but at the same time one nation.

Respect for humans still lingered in Coyote's instinct but was overlain by fear and puzzlement. What had changed? Coyote was still coyote.

Coyote's dreams were interrupted when night came again with its protective cloak of darkness. She would lick her sore paws, soothing them with her warm tongue for just a moment's time. Once up, she would allow herself the great pleasure of a long, long stretch inside the protection of her hidden refuge. This enlivened her, getting her wild canine blood surging through her body once again. Standing in the darkness, she would again feel pangs of hunger. She was traveling through a strange land. In her family's territory she had known where to find food; now she had to search much harder for a meal. And it was winter. As she traveled, she kept her vibrant ears attuned to the movements of small rodents under the snow. Each time she discovered a mouse, she would do the coyote dive, the ultimate pounce, and quickly eat her snack.

As she trotted along under the iridescent moon of the thirteenth darkness, the open fields dropped behind her and human structures came into view ahead, some with lights burning inside. Roads crisscrossed the landscape. *What is this?* she wondered. At first she could give each isolated structure a wide berth, but as she traveled, the buildings drew closer together, separated only by narrow openings. Lights on poles began to line the roads, each one flooding the ground beneath it in a pool of illumination. Coyote's cloak of darkness became harder to maintain. The soft snow that had cushioned her sore paws turned into hard pavement that burned with a strange-smelling chemical.

Two bright lights mounted on a noisy, fleshless beast came toward her. Frightened, she ran between two buildings and peered out as it sped by. Her nose and her coyote sense told her that these structures and lighted beasts were human things. *Even during the night these humans are out!*

She heard dogs barking within darkened structures. *I cannot live here,* she thought. *I must keep traveling and find a place like home.* But how would she maneuver through this territory? She tried to remember what her mother had taught her about navigating such a landscape, but she could not. Her coyote knowledge told her only that now, here, she must be more vigilant than ever.

She moved cautiously back to the road, all senses alert, but when another vehicle's lights bored through the night toward her, she knew she needed to find another route. She ran behind a row of buildings, hastily crossed another road, and ran between more structures. Then she came upon a quiet traveling path. She had discovered railroad tracks. This path felt safer; it ran in darkness, and she felt less exposed. Forcing her pace, she loped along the snow-covered tracks that took her between assorted human structures and distant lighting from flanking streets. She knew she must keep going.

Time passed, and she marked its passing by changes in the light. Finally, panting heavily, she stopped for a moment. Fatigued and hungry, she saw the first rays of daylight in the southeast. It was time to find a refuge, but where in this strange place?

She had no time to wonder. She felt the ground tremble beneath her and heard a shrill, piercing whistle behind. Turning, she saw a huge lighted beast bearing down on her, and she just had time to run behind an evergreen shrub as an early-morning train roared by.

Then she heard dogs barking nearby, and her fear mounted further. Her mother had taught her about her fellow canines domesticated by humans. *Beware!* She took off in a streak, flying over the frozen snow beside the tracks until a large grove of trees appeared ahead. It was separated from the tracks by a wrought iron fence that she slipped through easily. Once inside, she noticed how much more quiet this place was than the surrounding streets. Thick old shrubs and large trees provided shelter, and numerous stones stood upright throughout the open areas. She had entered an old cemetery—another human concept she did not know. But she sensed there was refuge here.

She found a thick, tangled shrub and wriggled her supple body under its gnarly branches. As she began to settle in, circling her body canine style, she heard a familiar call: *Caw, caw, caw,* and then again, *Caw, caw, caw!*

Crow, it is you, she thought. There was comfort in that call, for coyotes and crows have been companions for thousands of years, helping each other survive, co-operating in the hunt and sharing the success of their efforts. It was good to know that crow was here too. If crow could survive in such a place, she could as well. She curled herself into a snug bundle of golden fur and drifted into dreams. In moments she was transported from this place and time.

Her dreams took her again to the prairies of North America, the home of her mother's ancestors. Every fiber of her being was steeped in the ancient culture of her race, and her dreams took her there over and over again as she journeyed into her new world

There on the vast grasslands, coyotes had lived alongside proud nomadic human hunters. (They were the Comanche people, who once thrived in the harsh, dry savannas of the American West.) Coyotes would watch the men slay bison using only their fleetness of foot and their skill with bow and arrow. These human hunters left behind food from the bison for coyotes to eat. There had been mutual sharing then, as these people had long before learned their skills of hunting by watching the wild hunter, coyote.

As time went on, Comanches began hunting bison in a very different way. They rode upon swift and beautiful great beasts that seemed familiar to coyotes from some remote genetic memory. But with these horses there came also a new kind of men who brought a time of great change, ending forever the life that coyotes had known.

Coyote was abruptly awakened by howling winds outside her shelter. Though the protection of darkness had come again, she understood that continuing her journey in this howling blizzard would only sap precious energy. It was too dangerous to travel this night. She heard a little rustle under her paw—a mouse. Quickly cornering the creature, she swallowed her only food of the day. She kept her ears perked for any other rodent that might be sharing her wintry refuge with her. It was a night to rest, and her wise, wild spirit understood the necessity of it if she were to survive.

Curling herself into a warm ball of fur, she returned to troubled sleep. Images flashed in her consciousness from a time when the great bison herds that had once darkened the horizon were gone, and the Comanches themselves were hunted by the men who had arrived with the horses. Coyote families hid behind sage bushes and watched this unfold, sensing that the fate of the Comanches might be their fate as well.

As time went on, more and more humans invaded the coyote's world, bringing great herds of slow-moving large creatures that ate the prairie grasses that had once rippled like waves on the sea in the unencumbered winds of the open country. Other wild beings who had lived on the prairie disappeared. Wolves, whom coyotes respected as their larger competitors, vanished from the landscape.

Coyote awoke with a start. The calm quiet that surrounded her refuge was comforting. She lay there, her beautiful coyote face resting on her paws, wondering where such dream images came from.

It was midday, and she began to hear noise in the distance: the snow-removal vehicles of the city. On and on the noise continued through the afternoon, not stopping until the early evening. Soon it would be dark, and she would have to be on her way again. She was ready to travel, for her muscles felt stiff from lying so long in this cramped space where she was barely able to move. She knew the snow would be deeper now and the traveling more difficult and labored, but she must move on.

As darkness filled the sky, she squeezed herself out from under the snow-laden branches of the aged shrub. A wonderland of winter beauty delighted her golden eyes as she peered into the night. All seemed quiet. The fluffy snow that had fallen the night before was a foot deep, and she was forced to plunge through it. But outside the cemetery, the snow had been cleared from sidewalks and streets. She made haste. Though the traveling was easy, she was in a dangerous place.

Then she saw tall human structures ahead, much taller than any she had seen before. Rising high into the sky, lighted from top to bottom, these buildings were surrounded by vast, floodlit open spaces, unremitting traffic, streams of humans on foot. Coyote dodged in and out of alleys and side streets, avoiding the busier arteries, timing her dashes across open areas, seeking what darkness and shelter she could find.

She smelled the water before she saw it. And when she saw it, she recognized it as a great river, wider and faster than any stream she had ever crossed. Her inner compass was guiding her steadfastly east, and now she needed to cross this river. Her will to survive both pressed her forward and held her back.

Coyote could see sections of what appeared to be solid ice in the river, but it would not be safe to cross. Large chunks of floating ice crashed together and broke up in the churning water. Ice that was solid one moment fractured the next. Huge slabs piled atop one another, heaved by a powerful current. She stood motionless, eyes scanning the landscape, nose smelling the strange scents of the city. Her gaze rested on a massive structure that spanned the river a quarter mile upstream.

Nose high, sniffing the night air for clues, she moved slowly toward this structure. In the shelter of a stairwell behind a building near the bridge, she sat and waited, observing with her keen eyes. Cars crossed the bridge—many at first, fewer as the night wore on, and finally only one from time to time.

She needed to make a decision, and quickly. She made her final approach, and all was silent in the night. Without any question in her mind, she darted full speed across the bridge, her legs almost taking her airborne with a swiftness fueled by fear. Once across, she stopped for a moment and looked back to the world from which she had come, knowing that she would never return.

2

February 1970

There was no time to linger beside the mighty river she had just crossed. She must let the night surround and protect her and seek a more secluded route to travel. She pushed onward, and the city faded into the distance behind.

She knew well the dangers and agonies of trap and snare. One of her brothers had begun to venture outside their protected forest when he was only a year old. Though young, he was already an accomplished hunter, but there soon came a night when he did not return. His family found him several days later, bludgeoned to death after being caught in a leg-hold trap. Her parents had moved his body under a hemlock with branches low to the ground. After burying him under leaves and needles, her parents had left together and traveled to a remote corner of their territory to grieve. They had returned days later.

Already on her journey, she had seen members of

her own kind who had died ignominious deaths after being caught by these devices. Approaching them, she had seen agony frozen on their faces. Those caught in snares had slowly suffocated, the nooses of the snares tightening inexorably as they struggled to free themselves. Their beautiful faces had been distorted by intense swelling as the tight snares constricted their blood. Their obvious suffering had reinforced her will to survive. These fresh memories kept her in a state of unwavering caution.

The farther she traveled, the more confidence she gained in herself and her capacity to survive. This night was beautiful and clear, the stars in full splendor. Occasionally she stopped for a few moments and looked up at the sky. Coyote was comforted by the stars. They were the same stars that had delighted her in the protected forests of her home. She hadn't left them; they were accompanying her on her journey. To her they were like the crow: part of who she was, part of her culture and history. They gave her courage.

The deep boreal forests did not return after she left the city. Instead, the starry night permitted her to see once again the open fields and scattered structures in which humans and their domestic animals lived. This would not be a place for her territory—it would not be safe. So she pushed onward. Wherever there was a corridor of forest in which to travel, she sought it out.

When the changing quality of darkness told her that

daylight would be coming soon, she looked for a place to rest and hide. In a small clump of forest, in a thicket of shrubs and evergreen bushes overgrown and woven together like a wild quilt, she found shelter. There she would rest, exhausted from her long night's journey, her paws scuffed and sore. But first she must find food, as her hunger could no longer be ignored. A little stream, frozen over, meandered through this small patch of forest, and there she sought out mice. Her experienced nose found them swiftly, and she consumed them with haste. The meal was meager but sufficient to allow rest. She snuggled into the thick overgrown shrubs and fell asleep.

Her mother came again to her dreams, a comforting presence. Coyote's mother had dispersed from her birth family's territory and headed north, following the ancient wisdom of her kind. She had traveled a very long distance to find a new life. Though her journey had been perilous in many ways, she had been spared one danger: There had been no threat of wolves killing her as she skirted the edges of their territories, because the wolves were gone.

Yet the absence of wolves had itself been threatening in a way Coyote's mother could not have explained. Wolves and coyotes had lived side by side for tens of thousands of years, and coyotes' lives had been better because wolves were there. Coyotes are great hunters in their own right, but the bits and pieces of meat left from the wolves' larger kills—the bits coyotes were able to eat before the wolves would notice them and seek to chase them off or kill them—often saved coyotes from starvation in harsh times.

But wolves were gone from their former prairie home when Coyote's mother had made her journey; what was left was emptiness. Where once the wolves' powerful energy had filled the land, where once the cottonwood bottomlands had felt their commanding paws as they traveled together; where once their songs had filled the night, the land was silent. Their haunting songs were no more.

As Coyote's mother traversed a vast continent without wolf, somewhere in her wild being lurked a need to colonize a land left empty. She needed to fill the vacant spaces with her coyote presence. Her paws needed to touch forest floors bereft of wild travelers. She needed to end the lonely silence of the night, filling it with haunting song.

There was another motivation for her mother's continued traveling—a fear of men. As a young coyote she had hidden in terror as she and her siblings witnessed their parents being burned alive, screaming in agony. In order to protect their offspring, her parents had placed themselves as decoys, thus allowing their young ones to escape. The coyotes' life in the vast prairies would never be the same, so Coyote's mother had traveled on and on, eventually entering the cold northern forests, far from her prairie home. There, in the strange new world of the north, she had hoped to find another home.

Coyote was awakened by the sound of barking dogs. The dogs were coming closer. Terrified, she remained still, barely breathing, eyes straining to take in the approaching danger. Heavily panting dogs arrived just beyond her refuge, circling and barking, circling again. Her heart raced. She knew there was no way out. She would have to remain where she was, silent and still. Then she heard the voice of a human calling them back. Resisting the call, they kept circling.

She was frozen with fear but remembered her mother's unspoken thoughts when she was born in the deep, soft den of her forest home: *You are Coyote, you are Coyote. You will find a way to survive!* Her mother would then lick her tiny pup's muzzle and cuddle her under her warm golden fur along with her four siblings. Unable to discover her secret entry, the dogs finally gave up and trotted off.

It was afternoon. Hunger and thirst engulfed her, but not even these could drive her into the open daylight. Escaping her yearning for food, she fell back into a light sleep, dreaming of a time when she had been warm and safe in her parents' care. Her dreams took her back even further, to the time she was conceived in her mother's body.

Every sinew of her tiny developing being had been filled by the wild spirit of her mother's blood coursing through her. Her ancient ancestry was infused in her cells, so that she would know who she was and who she was to become. She could feel her littermates nestled close to her, traveling this same journey together, know-ing little of the world into which they would be born.

She could feel her mother's heartbeat, her breathing, and the gentle warmth of her body. Coyote could feel who her mother was. Her parents had handed down to her a legacy of ancient wildness and a capacity to survive against all odds. They had handed down to her the role she was to play on this earth, that of a carnivore, respon-sible for the health of so many other lives.

Her mother and father had given her this body to use in her journey through life. Her golden eyes would see the minutest details under her feet and in the far distance. Her ears would catch the busy activity of mice in meadows, along streambeds, and in their tunnels be-neath the snow. And nothing, ever, would be missed by her nose: not the smell of underground water in dry country, not the merest trace of possible prey, not the fragrance of sweet berries at summer's end, nor the odor of danger. Her long, agile legs would be capable of run-ning at high speeds and swimming long distances.

Her mother and father had fashioned a beautiful fur coat for her to carry through life, keeping her warm in the winter and protected from biting insects on hot summer days. They had given her a voice with which to sing her wild song and fill a silent, lonely land. They gave her a name from their ancient language, a language that has no words but is full of meaning. And they gave her a birthright of freedom. She was born to be free, that she might express her unique intelligence and beauty on the earth.

Abruptly she awoke from her dream into a profound loneliness. She missed the comfort of her family and wanted to reach out to her own kind, to find comfort in their company. She could not help herself. Sitting on her haunches in the cold night air, she raised her head to the sky and sang her coyote song of longing. She created her own unique song of yearning, sending it high into the starry night and back down to the earth again. But the only reply was silence, a lonely, empty silence in the night. She was truly alone in this strange new world. She must keep moving until she found her own kind once again, until she found her mate.

Her mother, too, had sung a song of longing as she traveled farther and farther into the northern boreal forest, a place so different from her former home on the prairie. Thoughts of her mother spurred Coyote on as she began to travel through another night.

One day her mother had sensed a different feeling in the air, something like the feeling of home. Wolves were there—she sensed them in a way that only coyotes could—but these wolves were different somehow. Though Coyote's mother did not see them, she felt that something about these wolves was like her. That is all she knew. She sang again her song of longing, and a low, haunting song responded.

The northland had been gripped by intense cold

when Coyote's mother arrived there, but nonetheless she was feeling a powerful inner drive to find a mate and become pregnant for the first time. And so she sang her song again, and once more the haunting song responded to hers, closer now. Then she saw him emerge from the forest and move toward her. He was a wolf, but not one of the bison-hunting gray wolves of her prairie home. He was smaller, and his thick coat of fur was filled with rich hues of red. He did not seek to kill her, but instead sought her company, sought her as his chosen mate. He was lonely, too. Coyote and wolf found each other in a world changing in immeasurable ways. They found a way to recreate themselves and bring a new, vibrant energy into a shattered world.

Coyote traveled onward through twelve more darknesses, traversing perilous open fields and narrow corridors of forest, avoiding towns, sheltering by day, finding what food she could. Then one night she stopped short. The starlit landscape ahead appeared dramatically different. The familiar, fragrant aromas of a northern forest began to fill her being as she took in long whiffs of its sensuous delights. She had arrived in a wild and beautiful land, akin to the home she had left behind. Though she did not know it, she had arrived in Maine.

3

Late February 1970

As Coyote entered the deep forest, signs of life began to appear, even in the cold of winter. Ravens were waking from their night's roost and calling to each other in their colorful language. The large paw prints of a lynx crossed her path, inviting her to follow. Her eye caught sight of a snowshoe hare that was hastily munching on fallen aspen leaves before seeking its hidden refuge for the day. Might this be the very prey the lynx was seeking?

Insistent hunger spoke to her once more. *Might there be a chance here?* Despite her exhaustion and weakness from lack of food, she approached the hare carefully, and then with a powerful pounce, jumped within inches of it. But the hare took off at lightning speed, leaping through the snow on its great snowshoe paws. Coyote followed with all the speed her long, slender legs would allow in the deep snow, turning and twisting as the hare darted in all directions. Yet despite the intense effort of every sinew in Coyote's body, the hare slowly put distance between them and disappeared into its deep hidden burrow.

Exhausted from the chase, Coyote stopped to rest. She could feel her heart pounding in her chest, and she was breathing heavily with her mouth gaping open, drinking air. *All for naught, all for naught.* She must find sustenance soon, for she felt herself losing strength.

Recovering, she moved on slowly, dragging herself through the deep snow. And just when she felt that she could no longer push on, her ever-keen sense of smell guided her toward the scent of a familiar prey, a prey taken when times are hard for the hunted as well as the hunters. There, not five hundred feet ahead, lay a deer that was still warm, having just died of starvation. Her coyote instinct informed her that this deer was safe to eat. It was not one of those placed as bait to draw her into a trap.

Approaching the first substantial food she had been able to secure since the start of her journey, she walked with elegant posture and gait despite her gnawing hunger and weakness. The ancient connection between predator and prey, fashioned over millennia, commanded respect and understanding. Death is not an end in the wild; it is a new beginning. Coyotes understand this.

First consuming the heart and liver and then the warm muscles of the deer's thighs, Coyote ate her fill, feeling a return of life and renewal of energy. Her sharp canines and powerful jaws were part of nature's design. Others in the forest relied on her to open the deer's body and would approach the carcass after her. She could already hear raven's hoarse and resonant croaks and cackles, alerting family and friends of new food nearby. Before she left the immediate vicinity of the deceased deer, her powerful jaws broke off one of the forelegs, and this she dragged away with her.

As the pangs of hunger subsided, she could finally sleep. She settled under the snow-laden low-hanging limbs of a large spruce and drifted off to sleep in the quiet and peace of the forest.

Her abated hunger manifested itself in dreams, and she again felt the safety and security of her mother's womb. There was no wanting before her birth, for her father watched over her mother, hovering over her and bringing her food when she finally entered her meticulously prepared den to await the birth of her pups. She had been digging it out for several days and then had plucked some of the soft fur from her underside to create a cozy bed for her pups when they came into the world.

It was chilly when the birthing day arrived, but life was beginning to abound in the forest of the north. Her father stood at the den's entrance, head lowered, straining to hear the first whimpers of his newborn pups. He gazed intently as he heard the soft cries—first one pup, then a second, then a third and a fourth and a fifth. Coyote was the third to move from the warmth of her mother's body into the unknown world. She had no sooner emerged than she felt the warm, comforting tongue of her mother licking her all over and then tucking her under her warm coat, where Coyote's tiny nose went immediately to work at the business of survival. She smelled her mother's milk, and she, along with her four siblings, drank for the first time the life-giving milk from their mother's body. Then, exhausted from the journey of their birth, all five pups snuggled tightly together in the warm embrace of their mother and went to sleep.

Coyote awoke from her dream with a start when she heard the sound of heavy footsteps moving in her direction, crunching through the cold blanket of deep snow. They were slow and deliberate steps, stopping for moments at a time. She stretched herself close to the ground and cautiously peeked out. At first all she could see were legs, four elongated legs. Her eyes strained upward until she had almost turned herself upside down to view who it was that had approached her secluded resting place. There, not more than twenty feet away—a familiar sight to her—stood a great bull moose. He towered motionless against the backdrop of this wintry forest scene, as though sensing her presence. He looked thin and weak but had an aura about him that spoke of his determination to survive. She watched him move slowly away, stopping frequently to gather his reserves of energy for forward progress through the deep snow. She would follow him, as he was creating an easier path on which to travel.

The days were getting longer now, and the midday sun felt warmer, suffusing her fur coat and enlivening her spirits. She must keep moving and find a mate, for she could sense that there were open territories here where no wolves or coyotes lived. Once she found him, they could establish a territory of their own and begin their life together. That evening Coyote placed her paws in the large hoof tracks of the moose and resumed her journey. She allowed him to lead her onward, not knowing where his path would take her.

The landscape became more rugged, with forested mountains and valleys unfolding ahead. It was a beautiful and magnificent landscape, but one in which survival would require extraordinary competence. There would be many small, flowing streams full of life as the mountains let go their snowy blankets to tumble down and feed the vibrant life in the valleys below.

On Coyote's second night following the moose, the tracks abruptly ended at what looked like a marsh—an open clearing with short, stubby branches barely showing themselves above the snow cover. There he stood, immense in stature, peeling the bark from the willows that grew in profusion along the marsh's borders. This was his sustenance in this late time of winter. It would help him survive until the fresh new greens of the marsh could strengthen his body once more. She left him there, grateful for the easier journey he had granted.

Coyote traveled on, wending a path beneath the great

pines and spruce and fir where the snowpack was thinner, saving energy any way she could during this time of food scarcity. She knew she must find a place to rest, as she was fatigued from her night's journey.

Eventually she came upon a beautiful frozen lake. It was letting go of the cold blanket of ice that had gripped its shores, and in some places the ice appeared to be getting thinner. This was just the sort of place that often abounded with her favorite and dependable food—rodents! Cocking her ears to listen for the scrambling of the little ones under the snow, she held herself stiff and motionless and then took off into the air with one powerful pounce to secure her quarry. Her parents had taught her well.

Hunger sated, she looked out over the frozen lake, and it brought back memories of the beautiful sunsets over her family's lake in their forested home. The lofty branches of the trees that bordered that other lake had held themselves as brilliant red sentinels for precious moments during the fading sunsets. The whole family would gather. Her father would begin his haunting wolf howls, and her mother would contribute her jazzy coyote yips. The pups excitedly voiced their glee with high-pitched little yips and yelps.

With these thoughts of home, a surging loneliness touched her deep within her spirit. She curled herself tightly in a snug circle of beautiful fur, covering her nose with her thick, bushy tail. She had always had her family around her for protection, support, and play. Now she was alone. When would she find her own kind again? The landscape seemed empty without her family's companionship and familiar songs. Thoughts of her happy puppyhood comforted her as she drifted into sleep.

She remembered feelings and sensations of her world when she was newly born. She remembered most of all the warmth of her mother's thick, beautiful fur surrounding her, the warm breath of her mother as she cleaned her so gently with her tongue, and the warm, sweet-smelling milk from her mother's body flowing through her. Her blue eyes of puppyhood had not yet opened, and what she could feel with her tiny body and sense with her nose had constituted her entire world. Whenever she whimpered a need, her mother responded with attentive solicitude. Her brothers and sisters shared this short-lived, euphoric time of their lives.

Their mother never left them, remaining tightly snuggled with her little ones, adjusting her body to the cramped space of their den. But she was well cared for, as her ever-attentive mate brought food he had hunted and left it at the den for her to eat. When he was not hunting, he stood guard, alert to any danger that might lurk. And danger was always lurking in their wild world, as predators of all kinds were well aware of the birth of the pups, though they were several feet underground in their hidden nursery.

In time the pups' blue eyes opened, and they glimpsed

their mother for the first time in their darkened nursery. Not long after, they saw her gently stretching her body upward, toward a light. The five pups cuddled together and watched her find her way out of the den. They could hear the excited greetings exchanged by their mother and father. Then they heard their father summoning them in a language only coyotes and wolves know. And so arrived the most momentous moment so far in their newborn lives. Coyote understood that she needed to be where her parents were, so she began clawing and scratching her way up, her siblings close behind. Father and mother, heads cocked, listened attentively for the approach of their little ones.

When she and her brothers and sisters finally found their way to the opening of the den, their mother and father were there to welcome them into the sunlight for the first time. Each one tumbled out onto the soft grass and delighted in leaping about and then toppling over, trying out their little legs, accompanied by excited squeals. What fun it was to freely romp about with each other as they scrambled in and out of their parents' legs!

Soon their exuberance melted into puppy sleepiness, and it was nap time. Before they curled up in the sunlight, all five pups mobbed their mother as she stood next to their father. When she nursed her pups outside the den, she did not lie down but stood, as she needed to be on guard for their safety. Knowing exactly what to do, her pups stood on their back legs, stretching to reach their mother's milk, each one supporting the other with their tenacious little bodies. When their tummies were full, they curled up in a snug bundle, one piled on another, and fell asleep in the warm afternoon sun.

Coyote's happy dream broke off with the sound of dogs barking. She was terrified; they had obviously caught her scent and were advancing quickly toward her. There was no hiding now; it was too late. She must run for her life, run with her long, powerful legs and her determination to survive.

She took off dashing beside the lake with the dogs close on her heels. When she could almost feel their breath, she decided to cut across the lake; though she had seen already that the ice was breaking up in spots, she must either risk drowning or be torn apart by the pursuing dogs. She raced across the lake as carefully as her speed would allow, her momentum and agility keeping her almost airborne over the ice, front and back legs meeting each other in midair as she strained forward.

The dogs followed, but soon she heard a high-pitched yelp and then a cry as one of the dogs broke through the ice and fell beneath, drowning. The other dogs stopped in terror, yelping and whining and backing off. Then she heard the human calling them back, and they quickly responded. She never looked back; her acute hearing told her all she needed to know.

Across the lake, still in fear of her life, she halted at last. She gasped, drinking oxygen deep into her lungs, her legs trembling from the intense speed of her flight. She had to stop, if only for a moment.

She must not stay, though. The yelping of the hounds grew fainter, but she did not know the intention of the human. She must keep moving and travel as far from here as she was able. Shaken to her innermost being, she made her way through a dense spruce and pine forest, remaining under the protective cover of the trees.

As she moved through the forest, she looked up and admired these great, tall beings. They were rooted deep in the earth, and their powerful trunks reached high into the sky. Like them, she had been born deep in the earth, and like them, her song rose into the sky. She felt comforted in their presence, felt the freedom of their tall spires, and when she passed close to one, she felt the tree's life connect with hers. She was part of this forest, and the forest was in her.

She traveled all day, not even stopping to hunt for mice. She was famished when darkness came on and she finally gave herself permission to stop and hunt for food. The scents of the melting landscape enticed her nose, and she passed some time seeking rodents just under the soft, melting snow. But weariness soon overcame her, and she found a snug, hidden space under an immense granite boulder and fell quickly to sleep.

Her dreams had been a place of refuge for her as she traveled farther and farther from home. As she slept, still feeling pangs of hunger and stabs of pain in all the muscles of her body, she dreamed of the comfort of her puppyhood and the first time her parents brought wild, solid food home for her and her brothers and sisters to eat. Their food had been kept warm for them in their parents' bodies. Before long, their father or mother would catch a mouse for them and set it down, encouraging them to begin honing their hunting skills. And as her blue eyes of puppyhood changed to a golden hue, she had felt her body growing and her legs becoming longer and stronger.

She watched her mother and father greet each other when one of them would return from hunting for the pups, for one of her parents always stayed behind to watch over the litter. When her father returned, her mother would wiggle her whole body with excitement and wag her tail exuberantly, tapping his fur with her forepaw and licking his muzzle. Her father, delighting in the affection of his mate, stood still and accepted her vibrant expressions with dignity.

Her parents were utterly supportive of each other in the care of their pups, and they would allow the pups a good deal of frivolity. She remembered her father's great gentleness to her and her siblings, allowing them to scramble all over him and sit on his back when he was resting in the grass. He was completely committed to the care of his offspring; in caring for them, he was safeguarding both his own wolf and his mate's coyote lineages. His pups carried an invaluable legacy of canine wildness into a world dominated by humans.

Coyote awakened as the rising sun again warmed her golden fur and sent delicious wild scents swirling around her. What was that movement? A hare hopped about nearby, on its way to its protective burrow as daylight emerged in the forest! Her hunger had not fully abated before she had fallen asleep the evening before, and now it reasserted itself with urgency. She remained motionless, not even twitching her ears, barely breathing. The hare drew near, intent on entering its burrow nearby. Then with one sudden, powerful pounce, she secured her prey, the hare not even having a moment to experience fear. There was no waste, no violence or cruelty. She consumed every part of the hare's body, taking it into her own.

Coyote felt renewed by her meal and lay down on a patch of exposed, moist, sweet-smelling grass, allowing herself to drink the warm sun into her body. With her front legs stretched before her, she played with a small branch of fragrant-smelling spruce, chewing on its bark with pleasure. She felt good in this new land despite its dangers, and she had been traveling too long. How she wished to find a mate. There was such silence here, without the songs she sang and heard at home. Why was that? She had such a yearning that she could not contain herself. Sitting on her haunches and raising her head to the sky, she let out a long, long coyote song. It was a song of searching, of summoning, of invitation, of longing.

In disbelief, she heard a response from far away. Yes, it was the call of her own kind; it seemed full of pain and yearning, but also welcome. For a moment she sat still, not sure she had heard a true response. Then she threw her head back again, eyes looking straight up into the morning sun, and sang her song again. She heard the same response. This was not a dream. The answering song, though mournful, was real.

She must seek it out! Off she trotted with her coyote gait, bopping along in great anticipation. She traveled through the morning, communicating as she went, wondering why the one who answered was not traveling toward her as well. And at last she found him.

4

March 1970

The moment she saw him, she understood why his song had been mournful and he had not come to meet her. He was in a small clearing, caught in a leg-hold trap. She was frozen with fear. Were there other traps near him, and would she fall prey to one of them? She could see that he had been struggling to free himself; the entire area around him was ripped up, the moist earth creating a wet mud that covered him and spiraled out over the snow. Blood was dripping from his mouth, revealing wounds he had suffered in his efforts to bite off the trap. His trapped leg was mangled, raw to the bone and spattering blood on his body and on the snow around him. He was frantic. There was fear in his eyes. He looked at her with longing as his body trembled with fear and pain.

Cautiously Coyote approached him, every step taken in fear that the same fate awaited her. She touched her muzzle to his and placed her forepaw on him, reassuring him that she was there to help. He understood, and they both understood that they needed to leave this place as quickly as possible. Both were aware of the fate that awaited him if he should be found in the trap.

She renewed his intense desire for freedom and survival, and he knew that there was only one way to freedom. He had to chew off his own paw.

With Coyote standing by his side, he gnawed off his bloodstained back paw, stoic in the necessity to do so. She watched in horror as he, with agony on his face, slowly released his mangled leg from the trap, his blood flowing onto the mud and snow. She had always been aware of these barbaric devices, and her parents had taught her to avoid the temptations placed near them, enticing them to approach. But until now, she had never watched her own kind suffer so intensely right before her eyes.

He won his freedom at last, but at a great price. He had been pulling so hard on the trap that when the last sinews of his paw were severed, he fell backward to the ground in a heap of shock and misery. She immediately began licking the stump of his leg with her warm tongue. Over and over she cleansed the raw bone, muscles, and ligaments of blood from the artery that would soon shut down its circulation to a paw that was no longer there. He lay still, barely aware of his surroundings, the nightmare and agony of his experience having sent him into an almost comatose state.

But she couldn't let him stay there. They must leave. Though his leg continued to bleed, she licked his muzzle, comforting him and bringing him back. She gently placed her paw upon him, encouraging him to stand. Slowly, while she stood close for support, he raised himself up, painfully finding a place of balance while keeping his mangled leg in the air. She knew that she needed to lead the way, to make decisions for them, to encourage him to survive.

A light snow began to fall. Before they commenced their journey together, she took in her jaws the paw he had been forced to amputate. As he watched, she carried it gently under the low branches of a spruce, and there she buried it under fallen needles and covered it with snow. They both understood that this precious part of his body needed to be left behind. She looked up at him, understanding his terrible loss. They must go. The falling snow would cover his bloodstained tracks and hers as well.

She blazed a trail, and he limped heavily as he followed her lead, weak from his struggle and in misery from pain. But he was coyote, too. He was a survivor.

His family's territory had been on the outer edge of the Algonquin Provincial Park forest. Traveling in and out of the forest's protection to hunt had been a very dangerous necessity. The previous autumn, when the leaves were changing color and the days were getting shorter, both his parents had been trapped and killed, leaving their two surviving pups to fend for themselves.

His sister, hearing her parents' cries of agony, had run in terror deep into the forest. He had searched for her, howling night after night, but there had been no answer. He had had to make the difficult decision to leave her as the cold winds were taking hold of the north country.

Compelled to leave that place of death, he had traveled east, just as Coyote had done, but his journey had been even more arduous, his traveling often hindered by snowstorms and bitter cold and hunger. Still, he had survived and had continued traveling, for no songs had responded to his song in the night—until now.

They traveled cautiously through the afternoon, stopping often to let him rest for a few minutes while she licked his wounded leg clean and warmed it with her tongue. In late afternoon, she encouraged him to curl up and rest under a protective ancient pine while she went hunting for both of them. Little rodents were busy traveling in their tunnels just under the melting snow, and Coyote's ears did not miss their slightest movement. Over and over she pounced successfully and brought him back a stomach full of mice and voles to eat.

When evening fell, they were both exhausted. They had pushed themselves as far as they could away from the dangers they had endured. They needed to rest, and his leg needed to begin healing. They found a small cave in a high granite rock wall overlooking the valley they were traversing.

There she would sleep with one eye open while he rested. Though alert to danger, she was able to sleep and find comfort in her dreams. If danger approached, she would awaken with a start. They curled together into a snug warm golden ball of coyote fur, tails covering their noses and his wounded leg, and slept.

The day's harrowing events brought forth in Coyote's dreams the tragic loss of one of her sisters when she was very young. Her two sisters, only two months old, were playing in the warm sunshine when a hawk swooped down and carried one of them off. Her father, always alert to the dangers faced by his vulnerable little ones, had chased away this same hawk three times when it was strutting around the den site, but the avian predator's fourth approach came so swiftly from the sky that Coyote's parents were helpless as their little one was carried away. They wailed through the night in grief.

Coyote awoke with a start as a great horned owl interrupted the night's silence with his resonant hooting—*Hoo, hoo-oo, hoo, hoo.* Then silence returned. Her gaze turned immediately to her sleeping companion, and she viewed his leg with concern. When he awoke, she would attend to his leg, cleaning it over and over again with her warm tongue. The light snow that had been falling earlier gave way to a clear night sky. They snuggled together in this magical night forest of the north. They had finally found each other.

This was the first day of their life together. Against

all odds, they had survived their separate journeys and found each other. They were among the first coyote pioneers to enter Maine, bringing with them not only their incredible coyote culture but also their wolf genes (for his father, like Coyote's, had been a wolf), restoring these to a landscape that had long been attenuated by their absence. The wolf had become only a distant memory to the people of Maine, for what had happened to the wolves of the West had happened likewise to the wolves of Maine—but many years earlier. This precious part of the Native Peoples' cultural heritage had been lost a century before Coyote and her mate undertook their journeys. Now these two young coyotes with their wolf genes trod the landscapes wolves had once traveled, drank from streams where wolves had once quenched their thirst, and sang to the mountains and moon that wolves' haunting songs had once serenaded.

Maine had been, for hundreds of thousands of years, home to a phenomenal diversity of life. But the landscape that met Coyote and her mate contained only a shadow of its past richness. The caribou that had once moved through the great northern reaches of Maine were gone. The wood bison and elk were gone; the flightless auk was gone; the wolf and the cougar were gone. The vast northern forest had been clear-cut and sent down the mighty rivers of Maine. The rivers had been polluted with the dioxin of the paper industry, reducing the numbers and diversity of the fish that had

once sustained the Penobscot, Passamaquoddy, Mic-
mac, and Maliseet tribes of the Wabanaki people—the
People of the Dawnlands—and many other tribes who
were no more. Generations of children had inherited an
impoverished landscape and knew nothing of what they
were missing nor of the potential this land possessed to
be enriched and healed again. Coyote had unknowingly
come to be a teacher for those who would learn. Her
very presence held the promise of renewal in this land
of the First Dawn.

Her mate awoke by fits and starts, whining in pain
and shaking with fear. Fear writhed in his memory, a
fear he could not yet shake. She licked his muzzle to
comfort him, her paw touching his shoulder to heart-
en him. She massaged his swollen and mangled leg with
her warm tongue, over and over. Feeling her comforting
attention, he looked upon her with affection and gratitude. He needed much healing, and this could not hap-
pen while traveling. They needed to stay put for a while
and attend to his wound. He needed to eat to regain his
strength. That they had traveled as far as they had the
day before attested to their will to survive—he moving
through his agony, she encouraging him.

The warm sun of late winter bathed them as a new
day began. All was quiet and peaceful in this forested
valley. Only the sounds of a woodpecker thumping his
beak in the crevices of a long-dead pine tree broke the silence. Soft wisps of gentle breezes fluffed their fur as they

cuddled close to each other, she moving his wounded leg to let it bask in the sunlight. They were both hungry, but only she could hunt, so she left him resting in their hideaway and picked her way down from its protective height. Everywhere she could see mouse tunnels in the thinning snow. Her nose followed them, alert to their scent. Over and over her well-learned hunting skills enabled her to catch her prey. When full, she found her way back to her mate and spilled out the contents of her stomach for him. He ate ravenously, as he had not eaten for several days before she found him.

As the days grew warmer and the deep snows diminished under the heightening sun, she continued to care for his wounded leg and then set out on her hunting forays, venturing in every direction. She found delightful small streams, freed from the cold grip of ice to bubble down slopes and over granite rocks covered with moss. The cold water refreshed her, and she wished that she could carry it back to him, but she could not. Here and there where snow remained, she saw lynx tracks again, recognizing that he had been traveling at high speed after a snowshoe hare. Unlike the lynx, she would obtain this prey through stealth, not speed. She would learn to use her wits and be as successful as the lynx in hunting this prey.

Every day found her mate a little stronger, his wounded leg slowly healing, closing in and reforming itself for the life ahead. After weeks of rest, Coyote found him standing and waiting for her, looking strong and alert, when she returned from hunting. He balanced himself on his three whole legs and just brushed the ground with the tip of his healing leg. He was ready. He wanted to move on and find their territory together. Though this was a beautiful forested valley, it did not feel safe to them. It was too close to the experiences of fear and pain that both of them had endured. But she made him rest a few more days before they resumed their travels.

With the morning sun guiding them east, they finally left his place of healing and traveled on, desiring to make the most of their one precious life together. They were on guard with every step. They sought a place where they would not have to be in constant fear of their lives, and something in their coyote wisdom told them that there was such a place and they would know it when they found it.

As they started down from their resting place, they heard a familiar and welcome sound of spring: *Ka-ronk, ka-ronk, ka-ronk, ka-ronk, ka-ronk.* The Canada geese were returning to their nesting grounds in the far north. What a splendid sight! The coyotes stopped and looked up at the large V of birds traveling overhead. Coyote misses nothing. Coyote delights in everything.

The sight and sounds of the Canada geese lifted their spirits, and they began to play with each other, tossing a stick from one to the other, then holding on to it together, playing a little tug of war. And she saw the lilt and shine return to his eyes. He was coyote, and coyotes delight in the adventure of life. This moment of frivolity did not last long, as the pain in his wounded leg forced him to stop, but the moment was treasured by both.

Onward they traveled until early afternoon. Then it was time to rest his leg and make sure it was clean. Under a large spruce with limbs that sagged to the ground, they snuggled together and went to sleep. As she lay there curled with her mate, she knew that her opportunity to become a mother this year had passed. Only during that very short period in the time of bitter cold, when her body's powerful hormones expressed themselves, could she have become pregnant, but she had been alone then and had missed the precious moment. There would be next year. First they needed to find a home, and her mate needed to heal—for she would need him when their pups were born.

She fell asleep, dreaming of the time she had witnessed her younger siblings, a year younger than she, scrambling out of their den nursery just as she and her littermates had done the year before. It was so exciting! They were so perfect and playful and captivating. It was her responsibility then to help hunt food for the pups, who were soon off their mother's milk and required their wild meat. She delighted in playing with them and graciously allowed them to tumble all over her, pulling her tail and nipping her paws. She would race around them while they followed in a tight bunch, whimpering joyfully as they attempted to keep up. She loved it all.

As the summer progressed, she had assisted her parents in teaching the pups how to hunt, standing over them as they pretended to capture a grasshopper or beetle. The pups were fascinated by anything that moved and would follow it intently and attempt to capture it with an outstretched paw. These experiences had prepared Coyote for the time that she would become a mother, but it would not be this year.

When she awoke he was licking her muzzle, an expression of affection but also of hunger. He could not yet hunt; the effort of pouncing on mice or chasing a snowshoe hare could undo all the healing that had taken place. She left him resting his wounded leg, and with the sun slowly fading in the late afternoon sky, she followed her ever-vigilant senses through the quickly melting snow of the northern forest.

Suddenly she heard thrashing in a stand of small spruce trees just ahead, and she crept carefully forward. There she saw a deer whose front leg was broken, the bone piercing her bloodied flesh. The doe was weak and emaciated, suffering from late-winter starvation and the excruciating pain of her wound. Coyote understood what to do. Death came swiftly as her canine teeth stopped the flow of breath and blood, and it was over. The suffering ended. The deer lay motionless. There was silence.

She needed to move quickly now, as the forest of late

winter and early spring was full of hunger. Because she had not traveled far from her resting mate in pursuit of food, she decided to run back to him and guide him to the deer's body. No sooner had they returned than ravens began calling out a proclamation to all those in the wild that food had been found! Coyote and her mate ate from the flesh and organs of the deer, taking her body into their own, and when they could eat no more, they took with them a portion that they could carry to their resting place.

They would return the next morning, but by then there might be nothing left. Possibly the bears had begun emerging from hibernation and would have heard the ravens' call. Night came, and the forest was alive with the calls of the hungry. Coyote had found food not only for her injured mate but for many others who counted on her to end the suffering deer's life and open its body. All through the night, those who would give birth to new life in the spring and summer would nourish themselves on the deer's flesh, preparing for future parenthood. Even the earth was rejuvenated, for as they fed from the deer, her blood flowed onto the ground and enriched the soil and the life that would spring from it.

Settling down at a safe distance from the night's activity, Coyote and her mate snuggled close to each other under the safety of a massive granite boulder, one of the many left behind more than ten thousand years before by a great glacier slowly retreating northward. There they rested, their starving bodies reinvigorated by the precious gift of another's life.

Coyote began to dream a new dream, a dream not of the past. She saw a place of mountain water running freely over granite rocks to form wild rivers that tumbled down wondrous waterfalls. She saw a great mountain rising from the pristine forest, with pure lakes dotting its base. She smelled the pungent smells of the wilderness once more and saw life in all its immense diversity emerging from the earth and swimming in the waters. Everywhere was abundance.

This was the most comforting dream of all.

5

April 1970

All was quiet in the early morning mist. The mild spring day was evaporating the snow that continued to cling to the earth, creating a milky curtain of moist air. Coyote lay peacefully, the soft fur of her head nestled against her mate's. She could feel his heart beat, and each breath he took mingled with hers.

She could still see the place of her dream—its mountains, rivers, and abundant life. Was it real? She knew only that they had not yet found their home, and she hoped it was near. She and her mate had traveled long distances to find each other. His leg needed to heal, and the need to keep moving was preventing this.

Her reverie was suddenly disturbed by the loud noise of powerful machinery. Her mate awoke with a start, fear on his face. Any sounds that came from humans immediately brought back the horror that he had endured. Both of them stood up, their muscles stiff and tense, straining their necks in the direction of the noise and foul smells of engines. They must leave immediately. They must not risk returning to what might be left of the deer's body.

Traveling cautiously under the protection of forest cover, they saw ahead a place of devastation. An entire section of forest had been cut down, ripped up, and hauled away. What was left behind were stumps of trees surrounded by caverns of torn earth. Life-giving roots splayed out in all directions, no longer capable of nurturing life. As they traveled east through the clear-cuts, they came upon numerous skeletons of deer who had perished in the winter. The clear-cutting had destroyed their wintering grounds, and they had found no protection from the cold and the deep snow.

Both Coyote and her mate had been taught restraint by their parents since they were young pups. Restraint was a matter of survival. They were taught restraint in their behavior toward each other, as Nature had given them the capacity to inflict great injury on one another with their canines and claws. They were taught restraint in their hunting and in how they consumed and shared what they hunted. They were taught restraint in their ability to bring life into the world, because only a certain number of their kind could survive in one place. What kind of restraint had been practiced here, in this place of desolation?

After traveling many miles, they finally left the clear-cuts behind and once again found themselves in the beauty and peace of the northern forest, surrounded by towering aromatic balsam firs and spruce mingled with great white pines, oak, maple, and stands of beech. These were by no means the virgin forests of long ago, but they were forests that were trying to survive, just as she and her mate were. Here they would rest, since her mate's leg had broken open and begun to bleed again after fleeing through the clear-cuts.

They spent several days resting and taking in the wonders of early spring. The migratory birds had arrived from the south and were singing their songs of territorial possession in the trees while wooing their mates. The woodcock wasted no time twittering its courtship songs above them. The forest was full of song! They lifted their faces to the heights of the trees, taking in all the life flitting about within those protective branches. High above them they viewed the red-tailed hawk soaring on windy updrafts, eyes peeled to the earth, searching for prey. Coyote notices everything.

Ah, and then they breathed the scents of a great lake. Their noses knew it before their eyes could see it. Their exquisite hearing confirmed its presence, too, for as evening came on, they heard the song of the loons, the haunting song of that water bird of the wild north. How that brought back memories of home to Coyote. There in the pristine lakes, the loons would fill the night with their haunting music, and her whole family delighted in joining in with their ecstatic songs, creating a symphony of wonder.

She could not help herself, and ecstatically joined the loons with her coyote song, sometimes jazzy, sometimes yipping, other times reaching the highest notes she could sing, holding onto them as long as her lungs would allow. And how could her mate not join in, for he too felt these same ecstatic memories? His eyes lit up, and he filled the night with his low, haunting wolf-like howls mixed with yips and yaps, expressing both his coyote and wolf heritage.

Their singing on this spring evening spiraled up to the sky from deep inside them. The full moon and the stars of every constellation received their song of joy, and all the animals of the forest perked their ears in disbelief. These were the spring nights of which they dreamed, for there is a place somewhere between appearance and fantasy where true life is lived, a place of wonder, majesty, and awe. This they experienced in this moment, and this moment was all there was.

After several days of rest and Coyote's attentive care to her mate's healing leg, they followed the intoxicating scent to the great lake. In less than an hour, they reached one of several pristine fingers extending from the long, expansive lake. The once healthy herds of caribou who shared this vast woodland and meadows with the towering moose must have frequented this place. Life was everywhere. Lines of slender merganser ducks in flight followed the winding courses of the streams that emptied into the lake, while blue-winged teal, black ducks, and wood ducks swam in and out of the marshes along its edge. Woodcocks hid among the brushy swamps, and vociferous killdeer pecked along the shore. There was a heightened sense of alert in all this diversity of life as Coyote and her mate approached the lake. *Has wolf returned?*

But as they trotted together toward the shore, all they sought from this unsullied lake was a drink of fresh, cold water. While they lapped up their drink with their long, pink tongues, they could see numerous fish swimming about, swishing speedily out of their way. The lakes were full of life. Refreshed, they looked up into the blue, blue sky of this sunlit day. The air felt warm and welcoming.

Coyote's mate looked at her, sharing his thoughts. She saw the gleam in his eye as he expressed his desire to swim from this shore to a small peninsula not half a mile away. The swim would do his leg good, and for him it was a better way to travel right now than struggling through the forest on his painful, healing stump. This lake finger had only recently been freed of its icy cover, and its waters were still brisk and cold, but that did not matter. With the gentle spring sun warming their fur, Coyote and her mate jumped in and paddled across, staying close all the way and looking at each other in glee. Each felt the other's excitement and the welcome feeling of weightlessness offered by the cold waters of the lake.

Soon they were on solid ground again. Ahead, to the east, was another small peninsula, again not a half-mile away across another finger-like extension of the lake. Though the great lake and its finger-like projections appeared natural, they were in reality the result of a series of dams that humans had built long before, transforming shallow streams with soft loamy banks into lakes.

Coyote and her mate gazed at the next peninsula, and the gleam in his eyes expressed his desire to swim there as well. He was recovering emotionally from his terrifying and painful recent experience.

They decided to rest awhile before their next invigorating swim, but first came the shake-down. Lake water flew out in all directions from their thick golden fur, reflecting shards of sun, as they shook themselves out, canine style. Delighting in these fleeting moments of comfort in their wild lives, they stretched out in the warm sunshine, gazing at each other in affection and slowly drifting away into a peaceful nap. For the first time since escaping the trap, the pain in her mate's leg had subsided. The cold water of the lake had numbed it just enough for him to experience relief.

No wonder he was ready for another brisk swim when they awoke an hour later. He stood ready, waiting for her to sniff around the tangled shrubs and early spring grasses near the lake for any rodents her nose might chance upon. And yes, up she flew in her coyote aerial display and pounced on her prey. One, two, and three times she was successful. And she shared the bounty with him, just a snack for the road, or in this case, for the water. They would need to hunt when they arrived on the other bank, as all this revitalizing exercise enlivened their appetites.

In another moment they leaped in, creating splashes that rippled out in all directions. As they swam, they viewed the distant shore excitedly. What lay ahead? Would it be the place they were seeking? As they neared the shore, they viewed a cow moose in the swampy wetland adjacent to the lake, but she paid them no heed, continuing her foraging of the early green shoots in the marshes and lichens on the newly exposed rocks. Never knowing what to expect in this new world through which Coyote and her mate were traveling, their senses were on high alert at all times.

It felt good to be buoyed by the supporting water while the afternoon sun glistened on the wavelets. They drank in a momentary sense of freedom from the struggles of their wild lives. As they swam, they noticed all the life swimming around and beneath them, especially when a sunbeam directed its shaft of light into the wondrous world below. They looked at each other knowingly, sharing the same thought—there is much food to be found in these waters as well. We will need to hone the fishing skills we learned from our parents.

They saw sleek creatures swimming at full speed beneath them, gulping down fish as they went. There were three of them, three adult otters that had come in from the river. They were so intent on their prey that they failed to notice the coyote mates swimming overhead. They were formidable predators in their own right, each one measuring three to four feet long. Having observed the otters' fishing technique, the coyotes would remember it and maybe try it themselves in time.

Emerging from the water at last, the coyotes stood side by side taking in the wild and sweet-smelling place they had reached. Their journey had been long and arduous, and it was good to be refreshed by the cool waters and the gentle spring sunshine. They shook themselves dry, then lay down to nap.

Again Coyote dreamed of a place where pure streams cascaded over marvelous waterfalls, and where a sense of abundance and safety reigned. Was there a place like that? When she awoke an hour later, her mate was looking into her eyes, resting his head on his golden paws. She sensed something he was trying to share with her, that he had a dream of this wonderful place, too. Something mysterious was coming to both of them in their dreams. They together were sensing in their dreams a place that could be home. And it was close, very close.

The silence of their unspoken communication was broken by a racket high above them in a balsam fir. A hungry martin was chasing a busy squirrel who had been so intent on jumping from one limb of the tree to another that she had not noticed the martin waiting for her until the last moment. She gave the martin quite a chase and escaped by the tip of her tail, jumping to another tree and scampering into her nest. Another hungry carnivore had been unsuccessful in the hunt. Watching this fast-moving scene unfold—for coyotes miss nothing—she and her mate were reminded of their own hunger. It was time to find sustenance.

Although the invigorating waters of the lake had deeply cleansed her mate's mangled leg and temporarily relieved his pain, Coyote would not yet let him hunt. He could not afford not to heal. They left their resting place by the lake and headed east into the forest, for it was already late in the day. As they traveled, they noticed thick stands of young fir and spruce, each tree vying with the others for survival. Their coyote knowledge knew who liked to hide in such places: snowshoe hare. They knew that, as evening came on, the hares would leave their hiding places to nibble on new growth.

Quietly they lay down in a thicket of young trees, their ears and noses alert to the slightest motion or scent. They waited and waited, stretching their faces high and sniffing the air. What is that? They held their breaths as an emerging hare came within two feet of them. Coyote pounced, but the hare narrowly escaped her jaws and took off. But he took off right into the front paws of her mate, who was standing now, watching every move. He quickly ended the hare's life, and it went limp in his grasp.

Something came back in his eyes at that moment,

something only a wild being who must take another's life in order to survive could understand. Coyote understood. He had participated in the hunt, and it had been he who caught their prey. He now realized even more fully that he was coyote and what that meant. He again remembered his name, the name given to him by his parents and handed down from his ancestors, a name not spoken, but who he was. He would survive, and he would help her survive.

Understanding this, Coyote wanted him to eat the entire hare. She knew he needed adequate sustenance to heal. He resisted and wanted to share, but she insisted that the hare was all his. Seeing that she would not relent, he voraciously ate everything, leaving nothing behind.

They traveled on in their bopping coyote trot, his gait slightly skewed. A small pond with wetlands around it soon appeared before them, and there she found rodents to satisfy her hunger. Both of them felt a powerful urge to move on. Somehow they sensed that this was the last day of their long journey; their destination was close.

Coming upon a road, they quickly crossed it. Each of them had approached many roads on their separate journeys. Then it had been winter, and few humans had been traveling on the roads; but a road always meant humans, and quickly crossing and traveling beyond it was important for survival. Coyote and her mate had both been taught this, and they did not forget.

They trotted along as the full moon moved through

the night sky. All was silent and still. Suddenly they stopped and looked at each other. A feeling had come over both of them at once, a remembrance of their coyote dream, the dream of a new home that coyotes understand.

They resumed their trot, then broke into an excited lope. Soon they found themselves surrounded by beautiful small lakes that shimmered in the moonlight. Diamonds and sparkles floated upon the waters, and loons began to sing their long, haunting melodies. This was it. This was home. They both knew it. And they turned their faces to the sky and celebrated in song, joining the loons in blissful chorus. They had found a wild and beautiful forest home where they felt safe.

6

May 1970

Now they could rest. Lulled by the mesmerizing sounds of the night forest, they circled in the customary canine way, settling down. Cuddled together, they soon fell asleep, but not before Coyote checked her mate's wounded leg and licked it clean with her warm tongue. Dreams came quickly, coyote dreams of refuge.

Grizzly bears had once roamed the Great Plains but had since been relegated to the mountains, where they found refuge. The wild mustangs that had originated on the American continent and later escaped the Spanish conquistadors to re-inhabit their former grasslands were likewise pushed to the most uninhabitable mountains for refuge. Coyote's mother had journeyed hundreds of miles to find refuge in a northern forest. The wolves, bison, prairie dogs, swift fox, golden eagles, and many, many more who had once shared the prairie with coyotes could find no refuge. Coyote culture retains this understanding. In Coyote's dream, her mother's silent wisdom spoke to her: *If you can, find a refuge.* Her dream ended there, but she knew, somehow, that she and her mate had found that refuge.

Coyote and her mate slept through the night and awakened to the delightful song of the sturdy little chick-adee: *Chick-a-dee-dee-dee, chick-a-dee-dee-dee.* And there, climbing head-first down a nearby great pine, was a white-breasted nuthatch. The forest was full of birdsong, and they could almost hear the ferns beginning to unfurl as the spring sun bid them rise from their winter sleep. Over there, along a rocky wall, a long-tail weasel was scurrying about, catching the scent of rodents and their hideouts. This morning activity of the forest reminded them of where they were. They were home.

They both bounced up and ran around in circles, smiles on their faces, playing tag with each other. Then they trotted off, for they had much to do. They had to let others know that this was their home. They had to learn everything about their new home and determine where the boundaries would be. That would take time, but what a pleasing time it would be. And equally pleasing to Coyote was to observe that her mate's leg was truly healing and that his pain was diminishing. He had gradually begun to support weight on his wounded leg and attempt to use it again.

Their ears perked up as they heard the alluring sound of a fast-running stream. Off they traveled in their excited trot, neck and neck, noses sniffing the early morning air, which was redolent with the verdant life around them. And there it was, rushing tumultuously, crashing into massive granite boulders that stood their ground, creating restless swirls of bubbling cold mountain water. As they trotted along the sometimes overflowing banks of this stream, they saw a tumbling waterfall ahead, roaring down over one huge boulder after another. Looking at each other in silent understanding, they both marked this spot. Now others would know that they had been here.

Just then they saw a flash of red that turned quickly off the trail ahead and hastened into the thick brush of the forest. Fox had recognized them and knew his position within the wild canine species. Coyote and fox would share this landscape now, each understanding the other's place in it. In the past, wolf had moved through these haunts, but wolf was gone now. Now it was Coyote and her mate who would fill wolf's niche, their paws touching the same moist earth, pine needles, streambeds, and marshes where wolf had once walked. And fox instantly understood this and knew how to be with coyote. It was a new beginning, and all those who lived here understood the change. The keystone carnivore had returned.

As they trotted along the tumultuous stream, Coyote and her mate were so enthralled by its fast-moving waters that at first they did not notice what was on the other side. Then they saw a road, partially covered by the last remnants of the winter's snow. That meant that humans could travel here on their machines, and if that were so, could this really be the refuge they had sought?

They quickly hid in a thicket near the stream, focusing their gazes on the other side of the road. There they saw a spectacular forest of fir, pine, maple, spruce, and beech, filled with birdsong. They could smell the moss and pungent decaying matter of the forest floor and all the new life beginning to spring up through it.

They looked at each other and made a wordless decision. The stream remained covered with an ice bridge where they were standing; they knew what they needed to do. They sprang up and gingerly crossed over the ice to the far bank, then raced across the partially snow-covered road, quickly seeking refuge in the forest. Once safely off the road, they stopped together and lifted their faces toward the majestic trees that sheltered them from human sight. These great trees were their refuge, and they felt safe under the forest canopy.

Coyote looked back at the dirt road. Its dwindling patches of snow showed no sign of human use. She looked at her mate's foot, and she thought, *Why should we struggle through the forest when this unused road appears to be safe to travel at this time?* Coyote looked at her mate, sharing her thinking, and her mate agreed. They began to trot north—upstream—with the riotous stream rushing past them on their left. But they were not alone. Almost immediately they heard above them the shrill, high-pitched call of a broad-winged hawk, newly returned from his winter grounds in South America: *Pweeeeeee, pweeeeeee, pweeeeeee!* As they trotted along, they were accompanied always just a short distance ahead by this winged guardian. What silent communication passed between raptor and coyotes as they traveled together? It was their secret, not to be known by others.

Cautiously the coyotes explored, she with her bopping coyote trot and he with his limping coyote trot, drinking in every scent and peering sidelong into the forest with their vigilant coyote eyes. Something was missing, or was it that someone was missing? Wolf is missing here; this is a place where wolf should be. Deep in her being, Coyote felt incomplete. Coyotes had always lived with wolves. Where were they now? Her mother had experienced that same sense of incompleteness while traveling through the prairies where wolves had once been but were no more. Yes, that is what she felt. She looked at her mate, then licked his muzzle, and he hers. Each understood what the other was feeling.

Soon hunger shifted their attention to the search for prey. They approached a place where several small streams that were flowing from the east, out of the mountains, joined the great stream that was rushing past them on its journey south. Here the broad-winged hawk parted company with them. Turning off the snow-covered dirt road, they traveled east beside one of the tributaries through a forest laced with numerous brooks. Before them scurried a banquet of small rodents. Coyote and her mate maneuvered up and down along the wet banks, hunting mice with their astute hearing and discerning noses.

Both their heads jerked up when a snowshoe hare ran by at full speed a short distance away. On its heels was a lynx, who had spooked his prey too soon and was losing ground in the chase. The lynx was too intent on his hunt to notice Coyote and her mate, but he would soon know they were there. After a meal of many mice, Coyote and her mate looked at each other again and spoke their silent, unspoken words of agreement: *We must mark this place as well.*

For this was another momentous place, the first place that her mate had hunted mice successfully on his wounded leg! No longer did his injury detract from his hunting skills. He would face greater challenges and more difficult prey in the future, and some day he would hunt for Coyote and their pups. But he was resilient, he was coyote, he would find a way. They left their scat on a large granite boulder—visible to all who should pass by.

They soon found themselves traveling along streambeds and beyond the high mountain range that cast shadows on the forest as morning drifted into afternoon. In a small meadow clearing, they looked up to smell the sweet air and saw in the distance a great mountain, still blanketed by the winter's snow on its peaks. The sight confirmed for them that they had at last found their refuge. This mountain would be a landmark for them when traveling through their territory. It would be the southernmost boundary of their home, and they would live in the sheltered valley beneath its great protective bulk. And when they sang their haunting wild songs in the evening, those songs would bounce off the high peaks and spread throughout the valley below. All would know that they were here.

The great mountain was sacred to the Wabanaki tribes—the People of the Dawnlands. They never called it Mt. Katahdin, but only Katahdin – "Our Father"—and they never sought to conquer it by climbing its peaks. Coyote did not know how significant her presence and that of her mate would be for this landscape and its people. Could there be a more poignant historical moment for a Native American people whose land and sacred mountain had been taken from them? Coyote and her mate had found their way to this place when the tribes of the Wabanaki federation—the Penobscots, Passamoquoddies, Micmacs, and Maliseets—were raising their voices for the return of their lands. Was not Coyote a sign of the healing that was possible for these tribes? The Native Peoples of the prairies would understand the immense significance of Coyote's arrival.

Those who displaced the Native Peoples from Maine thought the dispossessed would disappear, but they did not. Instead they have come back with their own voice, honoring their culture and the landscape their ancestors lived on for centuries. So, too, men with guns and traps and dogs have attempted, and continue to attempt, to eliminate coyotes from the American continent where they have lived for millennia, but coyotes have survived and will make their voices heard through the next millennia, their song a haunting totem of life fierce for continuance.

The following days brought onslaughts of black flies, those tiny flying signs of spring in the north. Black flies possess a precise clock that ticks in unison with the changes of the season, and the obnoxious pests arrive right on time every year. Along with their overwhelming swarms came an awakening of myriad forms of life, all of them comingling in a dance of diversity. The numerous crystal-clear streams bubbling over granite rocks and pebbles provided welcome places for the coyotes to play and relief from pesky insects and from the heat of the sun on their thick fur coats. Splashing about in these refreshing waters, they could see small fish dodging their playful paws in a game of catch me if you can. By midafternoon on sunny active days like this, they were ready to nap in the shade of a great pine. Snuggling together, they dreamed the dreams that coyotes dream, the ones only they know.

But what was that sound pulling them from their dreamy reverie one afternoon? No, it could not be so, this was their refuge. But it was so. They heard the sounds of human voices. The voices were coming closer. *Let us run. No . . . let us hide!* And so they nestled close to each other, hidden in the forest cover.

The humans approached, four of them! But they had no guns, they had no traps, they had no snares, and they had no dogs. They were not there to kill. Perhaps they were seeking something else. They came and they left, leaving Coyote and her mate in peace.

All predators knew that wild fawns were born to their mothers at this time of year. Hungry bears, who had come out of hibernation not long before, aggressively sought out the fawns hiding in the tall grass while their mothers were feeding at a distance. The bears would end their lives swiftly and carry them away. Coyote and her mate were hungry and underweight after a long winter and spring of arduous travel and traumatic experiences. They were not to be deprived of this early summer sustenance.

The scents of new life guided them to their prey, a newborn fawn hidden in a nursery of tall grasses. In a split second the fawn, born to live with scores of predators, sped away in a burst of flight. That ancient, evolutionary relationship of predator and prey is Nature's design, the course taken through the ages to create balance and diversity, freedom from disease, and the continuation of the fittest genes in each species. Predators forced deer to become fleet and sleek; deer enlivened predators with gifts of keen intelligence, prowess, canines, and claws. The fawn that sped away before they could touch her would be the one to carry on.

Hunger is the wild carnivore's constant companion. It was hunger that drove Coyote and her mate to hunt and to sharpen their senses. So they moved on, again seeking relief from their hunger. Not long after, a whiff of new life came to them once again. This time they used their wit and the tricks of hunting passed down by coyotes through the centuries. Coyote's mate made a slow, wide circle around the fawn and settled himself down, waiting. Then Coyote slowly approached the fawn, knowing that it would spring up and run from her. And so this fawn, not thinking quickly enough, ran right into her mate, who ended the fawn's life instantly by grasping her neck with his canines.

There was no hate, no anger, nor intent to make another suffer; there was only the desire to survive. This fawn died, but she would live again in the coyotes. While the fawn was still warm, Coyote and her mate shared the body together. Nothing was wasted or left behind, not even the last drops of her blood on their fur, for they licked clean their paws and muzzles as they sat resting. The fawn's mother paced anxiously at a distance, understanding full well her loss. She then moved slowly away but would return later that day to breathe the last scents of her fawn's body. She also harbored no hate or anger. She understood and accepted the prey's ancient relationship with the predator in a manner only wild ones comprehend.

Their hunger abated, the coyotes curled up together as night fell over the forest and listened to the peepers in a wetland nearby, the hooting of the barred owl before it swooped down in silent flight from his perch on a great oak, the quiet movements of little creatures scurrying about in search of sustenance or cover, and the soft, comforting breezes of a mild spring night. Soon their eyes closed in peaceful sleep, a rare gift to a coyote.

7

June 1970

Coyote and her mate awoke with the sun in the land of the first dawn, fresh and ready for further adventures. But first there came that energizing canine stretch. Uncurling themselves from sleep, they stood and faced each other with smiles of affection, and with their forepaws extended, stretched their front legs out and then drew back from the tips of their tails. They held themselves in that refreshing pose, noses high, drinking in the myriad scents of the awakening forest. Then how could they resist a few moments of play? They began running in circles and leaping over each other, then discovered an unusually shaped tree branch to chew on together.

They lived completely in the ever-present moment, for how else could they survive in their difficult lives? Then off they trotted to explore their new home. In time they found a small path that made their travels easier, so they left behind some scat to be found by others who might come that way, letting them know that coyotes had been there and this was their home.

No sooner had they left their scat than they heard approaching human voices. By scent and sound they knew there were no dogs with the humans, and one of the voices was young. Scampering hurriedly into the forest cover, they found shelter and gazed out curiously.

There they were, three of them—one with a gentle voice, one with a deeper voice, and their puppy, their human child. The adults walked right past the scat, stopping a short distance away to take in the view of the mountains, but the child stopped and crouched down to wonder who had left this. His eyes were aglow with excitement, and he was so enthralled that he sat down on the path by the scat. Coyote looked at her mate knowingly—the child sees all! Just then, the child peered into the enchanting forest and saw Coyote and her mate sitting there, delighting in the child's wonder, just as canines delight in the play of their own pups.

Their eyes locked for a fleeting moment, and the child let out a squeal of delight as Coyote and her mate took off in flight. "Mom, Dad, I saw two doggies! We were looking at each other." But his parents took his small hand and said, "Eddie, dogs aren't allowed in this park." The child replied, "But I really saw them. They were beautiful, and they had no collars. They are free! See, they are right there."

But by then Coyote and her mate were far away from the trail. Eddie's mother said to him, "There is no one there, but we know how nice it is to make believe in the forest." And with that, all three of them continued their hike up the path toward their campsite. Eddie would never forget that experience, for in time he would come to know that he had spent precious moments with two wild coyotes.

Trails like that one must be made for humans who come here, Coyote thought, so we must use caution when traveling on them. But they are a good place to leave our scat!

Having seen humans twice within a short time, they decided to seek a more remote area. It seemed to them that no matter where they traveled, they encountered humans. They were everywhere! Even though the humans they had met in their new home had not sought to harm them, Coyote was wary of them and wanted to keep a safe distance at all times. Instinct and their senses directed them north. They traveled toward the center of the park, the area most remote from roads and least traveled by humans.

The ravens of the forest were by this time busy caring for their young, who begged incessantly for food. While searching for sustenance, a male raven discovered the two coyotes making their way along a small stream that meandered from a serene pond.

It was a fine summer day, and the two coyotes had

lingered by the bubbling clear water for a refreshing drink to cool themselves and quench their thirst. They played in the stream, splashing about and attempting to catch small crayfish and minnows, more for fun than for serious hunting. Raven, like coyote, misses nothing. *Has wolf returned?* the raven wondered.

The raven jumped down on a low branch of a great maple, just above where the coyotes were playing, thinking, *Hmmm . . . I'm not so sure this is wolf.* Raven's culture was an ancient one like coyote's, and there came to him the recognition of a wild canine that the Native Peoples had once honored and his ancestors had admired for their hunting prowess. The canines of ancient raven culture were survivors. Might these two be those special wild canines? If so, he would want to associate with them!

He jumped down to the ground ten feet from where Coyote and her mate were playing in the stream and let out his raven's croak: *Cr-r-ruck, cr-r-ruck, cr-r-ruck!* In response, Coyote and her mate let out their yips and yips and yips, standing in the stream dripping wet. Coyotes recognize ravens as colleagues with whom they have worked in the hunt for millennia. These two wild beings—one of the forest and one of the sky—understand each other in their journey of life.

At that moment the young raven chicks began an urgent clamoring that their father could not resist. Off he flew, his broad, shining outstretched black wings lifting him up into the trees, and he was gone.

It was time for Coyote and her mate to end their play and move on to discover and mark their territory. After splashing out of the stream, and before shaking themselves out, they walked over to where the raven had been standing and sniffed the ground. They would remember him now.

With the heat of late morning came swarms of flying insects, so the coyotes decided to follow the small streams in their path, knowing they could find quick refuge from greenheads, mosquitoes, and black flies whenever needed. Refreshing, cooling, pure water was everywhere. Fish swam through and around the many bubbling, miniature waterfalls created by boulders of all sizes and shapes that were scattered along the streambeds. Coyote and her mate trotted in and out of the streams, their ancestral ability to seek out the hidden waters of the dry prairies unneeded here. That never-ending search for life-giving water had honed the senses of her ancestors, one more manifestation of the remarkable resilience of her kind.

The challenge of these coyotes was not to discover hidden water but to adapt to a new and different world—and to figure out new ways to survive. And one of those new ways was to fish. Both of them had been taught how to fish by their parents; now it was time to hone those skills. Brook trout, the native fish of northeastern America, were visible everywhere they looked, and these speckled, multicolored fish can easily grow to thirteen inches long by the time they are three years old. A single fish of that size would be a substantial meal. So they watched for movement in the water whenever they stopped and sat along the stream. They knew they had to be very still and then leap into the stream quickly, surprising the sturdy fish by biting down on them with their canines. In due course, their well-learned fishing skills made for a successful catch, and lying next to each other, they enjoyed their freshly caught trout.

In mid-afternoon, tired by the early summer heat and the day's exercise, they curled up under the shade of a great beech tree for a nap. They awoke to a chorus of insects, each kind singing in its own key and rhythm, filling the evening with a vibrant beat of life. The sky was bright and clear, with the full moon lighting up the forest around them, throwing shafts of light through the great pines, maples, and oaks.

What is it about the full moon that makes coyotes want to sing to her? We humans have not yet been able to fathom their intimate bond with that distant child of Mother Earth that is bathed by the brilliance of the sun. Maybe we are not meant to know, but just to witness in wonder.

Coyote and her mate stood in the early summer night, illuminated by the magical moonlight and surrounded by an insect chorus that was waiting for them to join in. Their faces reached to the glowing sky, eyes mirroring the light of the moon within them, and they began their longing howls and joyful yips, their voices twirling in and out of each other's, spiraling higher and higher toward the moon. Their song filled the night air and traveled through the forests and streams, into the highest treetops, echoing from mountain peak to mountain peak and back again, that all might hear it. All life felt it, and the mountains remembered it.

And those humans at their campsite that evening heard the song as well. Sitting bolt upright in their tent, the parents of the little child who had studied Coyote's scat much earlier that day looked at each other in wild amazement and wonder as the hairs stood up on the backs of their necks. Their child, too, sat up bright and alert, eyes filled with excitement. "Maybe that is the song of the doggies I saw earlier today," he said. His parents sat motionless, transported to a realm they never dreamed they would experience. "See, I told you I saw two doggies!"

What went through those campers' souls on that summer evening in a wild forest of the north? Maybe they would never express it in words; maybe it cannot be expressed, but only experienced. They had heard the voice of wildness—the soul and spirit of wildness, free and self-determined—through wild beings expressing themselves in their own voice and their own language. The next day as they hiked back, these humans walked differently down the trail, experiencing this place in a whole new light, enraptured by unseen wild beings who had spoken to them.

Early the next morning Coyote and her mate left the vicinity of those hikers and traveled deeper into the park's interior. In the quiet morning twilight they had managed a successful hunt of two snowshoe hares using their coyote wit to corner the swift-footed animals that were abundant everywhere in the park. Coyote's mate would lie in wait while she maneuvered their prey to the desired destination. It was she who continued to take the more active role in their hunting, as they protected his healing leg from further damage. In time the leg would toughen itself against any reopening or infection, but his coyote trot would never be the same, and the memory of his loss would remain buried deep inside him.

By noon they had found their way to a tumultuous, fast-running stream that was forced into chaotic splashes, overfalls, and eddies by the large granite boulders in its bed. The roar of the cool water crashing off the rocks and rushing onward overwhelmed all other sounds of the forest and brought forth the countless scents of life welling up along its course. The torrent was a living being; the heartbeat of life pulsed through it as it swiftly journeyed, never stopping or tarrying. Their coyote spirits were enamored of it, breathing the exuberant life of the stream. This was a place of coyote dreams.

They delighted in pressing their noses to the damp earth beside the streambed, breathing in the moist fragrances of life unseen by the naked eye. This was a place they wanted to imbibe. So they rested there, hidden beneath the forest cover that extended to the edge of the stream. Late in the afternoon they roused each other, for they knew they needed to claim more of their territory, their new home. Before they trotted off, they left their scat on a granite rock, letting any others know that Coyote and her mate had been there and that this was now their home.

Their journey took them in early evening to a beautiful pond. They could see the mountains towering in the distance beyond the unbroken forested landscape that surrounded it. The sun was low on the horizon, casting shadows along with brilliant red and orange shafts of light to float on the pond, creating a scene of wild wonder. They were hungry, and both of them sensed the whiff of life.

An adult deer was foraging on the edge of the forest near the pond, and Coyote and her mate knew there must be a fawn nearby. Glimpsing a fawn that was poorly camouflaged, they carefully planned their hunt together, communicating silently and flawlessly. Again, she was the one to initiate the chase. The fawn fled, first stumbling to her feet but then recovering and taking flight. But those few moments of hesitation gave Coyote's mate time to make his move. Swiftly and precisely, he ended the fawn's life. There was no time for pain and only moments for fear.

The fawn's mother, hearing the scuffle, leaped anxiously toward her fawn, attempting to kick Coyote and her mate with her powerful hooves. They backed off, knowing that the doe was capable of dealing them a fatal blow. She stood over her fawn, touching the small body with her nose and hooves, panting and snorting in distress and grief.

But she had had twins that year and knew she needed to protect her second fawn from the same fate. So she slowly moved away, looking back one more time. And yes, she found her second fawn motionless and well hidden in tall grass. This was the fawn that would survive to adulthood and pass on her vigorous genes and powerful will to live. The mother and fawn ambled away together, more cautious and alert after the encounter that brought back memories from long ago of her own ancestors' lives with wolves. And she understood.

Coyote and her mate then returned to the fawn's body and shared it. Their fathers' wolf genes had given both coyotes even more powerful jaws with which to break bones than a prairie coyote possesses, so nothing was left behind. They ate the nourishing food knowing that the window of time in which to procure it was brief. The fawns that survived bears, bobcats, and disease would soon grow up to present a formidable challenge to a coyote, one not worth the danger of hunting. Nature has decreed that there be a short window of success for the predator and vulnerability for the fawn, and that window would soon close.

Evening was approaching, and the darkness of the north woods would soon fall over the forest. To free themselves from biting insects, Coyote and her mate plunged into the pond. They enjoyed swimming in ever widening circles around each other, then paddling along the edges of the pond to investigate everything they could discover. Invigorated, they raced ashore, streams of water dripping from their coats.

They felt safe, as safe as coyotes can feel in a world where many humans seek to kill them. The pair rolled onto their backs next to each other, paws relaxed and eyes glistening as they looked up at the clear starlit sky, where the billions of stars of the Milky Way created a magic coyotes have been delighting in for millennia. For some time they remained motionless, transfixed and peaceful. When they rolled onto their sides, Coyote noticed lights not from the stars, but from across the pond. She and her mate looked at each other, knowing that tomorrow they would find the source of that light. Then they drifted off to sleep, listening to the myriad insects creating a night chorus that hummed them into their coyote dreams.

In the morning twilight before dawn, they were awakened by a chorus of birdsong all about the pond. Each bird was singing its own song, but somehow they all sang together. The Eastern wood pewee with its beautiful little whistling sounds, simple yet exquisite; the great crested flycatcher with its loud whistled wheeep; and the warbling vireo with its excited calls joined the many other songsters in the trees. The singers were often unseen, but here and there the coyotes would catch sight of silhouettes flitting from one tree to another as the light imperceptibly strengthened and the early-morning activity of the songbirds heated up.

As Coyote and her mate took a long feeling-good stretch and shook out their fur, they looked at each other knowingly. *Today we will find out where that light was coming from last night.* Coyote curiosity is both a survival tactic and an indication of keen intelligence. They needed to know about that light, for it had not been a part of the night's natural setting. Before leaving to journey around the pond, they took a long, refreshing drink of pure cold water, their pink tongues lapping it up as their vigilant eyes watched for any movement in the pond.

They trotted off with their destination in mind, and had not traveled far when they were startled and frightened by the sudden flush of a ruffed grouse that had been hiding in the forest understory. They took off at high speed, front legs stretching forward and back legs straining to catch up, propelling themselves airborne for moments at a time. At a safe distance they stopped, turned around, and studied where they had been. *It was one of those grouse again!* they thought.

After standing quietly for a few minutes to catch their

breaths, they noticed busy activity under the leaf litter. With their noses riveted on their prey, they went airborne again, pouncing directly on unsuspecting rodents. Voles, mice, and chipmunks are everywhere and constitute an important prey for coyotes through most of the year. Though they are small, rodents often carry disease bacteria in their bodies. Coyotes are an apt predator to manage rodent populations and the diseases they can cause.

Meandering through the cool forest, the coyotes circled the pond. They saw a female moose and her young one feeding in the bordering marsh, and as they approached, the adult lifted her head from the water, a large bunch of fresh greens dripping from her mouth. Her calf, sensing his mother's alert behavior, directed his eyes where his mother was staring intently. Coyote and her mate stopped, too, and all four of them stood still in the morning coolness and stared at each other.

There was a knowing in their stares. The mother knew that she was safe and could keep her calf safe, and Coyote and her mate knew that as well. They all understood. The mother of the calf went back to foraging in the water, her calf following suit, and Coyote and her mate went on their way.

Late that morning, they began to feel the heat and humidity of the day, and annoying, biting deerflies swarmed around them. They jumped into the pond together, dog paddling in increasingly large circles around each other and, at the same time drinking sips of the refreshing cool water. As they swam, they could see numerous brook trout swimming below and around them but always swiftly swishing away when Coyote and her mate came too close. Once refreshed, they decided to sit motionless at the edge of the pond and watch for any trout that came close.

Just as they were beginning to swim toward shore, the antlers of a large bull moose emerged from the water close by, creating undulating waves. He had fully submerged himself a short distance away, foraging for greens in the water below. The three of them looked at each other in surprise—the moose with his mouth dripping fresh greens, and Coyote and her mate wide-eyed. This was by no means the first time they had come upon a moose, but the surprise of this encounter had caught them all off guard.

Mutual respect between moose and coyote runs deep in both species. The situation demanded that each keep a safe distance from the other. As the moose stood there staring at them and munching the greens in his mouth, Coyote and her mate swam hurriedly to shore, looking back over their shoulders as coyotes often do when fleeing a situation they consider dangerous.

Once back on shore, they were not going to let the moose deter them from fishing at a safe distance. Soon the moose began to move slowly away in search of more fresh greens, his massive body displacing the water around him as he stepped out of the lake and headed to the verdant marshes nearby.

Time passed, and no trout appeared. But they were coyotes, and it is the patience of the predator that keeps coyotes alive. More time passed, and then! A small group of trout ventured near the edge of the pond, seeking the coolness of the shade it offered. Each of them pounced, and each caught a trout! This was a meal, as each of their catches was nearly 13 inches long. This forest pond teemed with food for the trout; the surrounding forest drained its vital debris and nutrients into the pond, bringing a continual supply of food to the smaller creatures on which the fish depended for food. The coyotes hungrily consumed their catch of this colorful speckled fish, pleased with their fishing.

Hunger abated, Coyote and her mate felt the need for a long afternoon nap, as this summer day was becoming increasingly heavy with humidity, making it uncomfortable to exert much energy. Rain was on its way, and late in the afternoon, it came down in torrents, accompanied by bolts of lightning and loud cracks of thunder that echoed from one mountaintop to another. They found a grove of old white pines and settled under them as the storm raged. Rain continued into the evening, drenching all life that moved about in the forest. The coyotes too were drenched, but their thick outer fur protected their inner coat to some extent. Nature had provided for them. This was a coyote's life, and the forest was a coyote's home.

Night came, and again they observed the lights on the pond. Their travels this day had brought them much closer. With just a soft mist in the air now, they traveled toward the lights and hid in the forest cover to figure this all out. Then they heard human voices and smelled their scent, and imbibed the aroma of food cooking over open fires.

Coyote and her mate had already considered that those lights were from humans. Now that was confirmed. But both of them felt somehow that these humans were not there to hurt or kill them. They moved far enough away to feel safe, then settled down to sleep.

8

July 1970 to February 1971

The heat and humidity of summer were oppressive and uncomfortable to Coyote and her mate, who could not shed their thick fur coats. So were the ticks, fleas, and swarms of winged insects. Vigorous scratching often dislodged embedded ticks, and the pair would assist each other in removing them from hard-to-reach places. The cool, refreshing waters of the streams and ponds provided relief from these discomforts of summer in the north woods. They traveled close to waterways as they worked to complete their territorial boundaries, leaving scat and squirts of urine on rocks and other chosen sites, announcing to other coyotes that this was their home. Those traveling through would understand and move on. Right now there were no others, but in time there might be.

Traveling north, they approached several small ponds, some not much deeper than a marsh. There they recognized the work of nature's engineer, the beaver. Beavers had been eliminated from most of their range in the 1800s, when they were trapped for the lucrative trade in their pelts and the building materials for their dams—trees—had been destroyed by extensive clear-cutting. But now the forest was recovering in this protected landscape, and beavers were free to go about their dam building once more. Their engineering feats created ponds and lush habitat for a profusion of wild mammals, fish, amphibians, and birds.

Coyote and her mate saw two beavers swimming in a pond; the beavers stared back, then slapped their broad tails vigorously on the water and dove down, wondering, *Has wolf returned?* Taking in the rich diversity of life around them, Coyote and her mate knew this would be a core area of their territory. Their future den site would be surrounded by this rich and varied landscape.

At midday they remembered how tasty the brook trout had been the day before, and again they observed plentiful numbers of trout in several of the ponds. Because the ponds were shallow, the two of them stood stiff and quiet in the clear water and scooped up passing trout with their canines.

After another refreshing swim and some happy jostling with each other, they ventured onward into the last area they would choose for their territory. They soon found their way along a remote lake surrounded by tall peaks that rose in stunning grandeur from its shores.

The lake was crystal clear with gravel beaches, and its deep waters seemed to hide the secrets of its ancient formation.

For a short time they cautiously traveled the rugged beaches, drawn onward by the murmur of a waterfall. The murmur became a roar where a small stream entered the lake; after stopping to drink from the stream, they followed it away from the lake. Not a hundred feet away was a spectacle of wild water cascading relentlessly over moss-covered massive boulders above them and spilling into a small pool that detained the surging water only moments before freeing it to rush again on its hurried journey to the lake. Coyote and her mate looked at each other with a gleam in their eyes. Approaching the shower of water, they allowed it to drench them, drinking in its powerful energy.

Refreshed, they found a shady spot near the lake to rest in the heat of the afternoon sun. Soon they were asleep, snuggled together with their wet fur emanating the wondrous scents of the life-giving water. When they awoke in the early evening, acrobatic swallows were scooping up flying insects from the myriads hovering in the still air. A great horned owl hooted its resonant call, *Hoo, hoo-oo, hoo, hoo*, and moments later swooped down to clutch its prey, an unsuspecting rodent exposing itself above the leave litter for just a moment.

It was time for Coyote and her mate to hunt again, for hunger had awoken them. They stalked mice while a magnificent sunset mirrored itself on the waters of the lake in red, yellow, and orange streaks. The encircling majestic mountains seemed to guard the rugged grandeur of this place for all time. When night came, the pair of them, their hunger abated, cuddled together as always to rest.

Though coyotes prefer to hunt during daylight hours, the lynx prefers the night. The lynx's favored prey, snowshoe hares, had by this season changed their pure white coats to brown, camouflaging themselves while they grazed on forest vegetation. The lynx moved silently past in search of a hare, and warily moved away into the night. The coyotes were aware of his passing but paid no heed.

The heat and humidity of midsummer slowed Coyote and her mate in the days that followed, and they rested more and swam in the lake to cool off. They could see ospreys diving for trout and arctic char and carrying fish back to their growing chicks in a huge nest high in a massive white pine that had died many years before. Quiet days melted away as the two coyotes slowly ventured around the great lake, leaving their marks on prominent granite rocks and along game trails. By late summer they had almost fully staked out their chosen territory. Every inch of their new home would become familiar to them in time.

A favorite place from which to view the wide expanse of their territory was a high bluff at the north end of the lake. It was their lookout spot, and they were content to sit there for hours, viewing all the goings on as far as their eyes could see. They could observe the landscape all the way to the great mountain in the south. It was as though they were studying every unique and special feature of their territory and filing a map in their remarkable canine memory.

Coyote noses seek out a favorite food in late summer, for they have a sweet tooth that must be satiated before the leaves begin to fall. A soft scent guided Coyote and her mate along a stream and a trail rarely used by hikers in this remote part of the park, and they found what they were seeking: raspberries! They ate ravenously while morning twilight dissolved into day, gently plucking each berry from its thorny cane. But they were not too preoccupied to watch for the black bears they knew would be coming for this late-summer treat as well, and sure enough, just as the coyotes were satiated, a bear and her cub approached. Coyotes and bears saw but ignored each other as they went their separate ways—Coyote and her mate back to the lake, and the bear and her cub to their berries.

Autumn brought relief from the heat and biting insects. The birch trees at higher elevations painted a spectacular panorama of gold, while oaks and maples mixed their brilliant reds and oranges with the blue-green conifers to create a striking autumn mosaic on the mountainsides around the ponds and lakes. As Coyote and her mate rested beside their favorite fast-moving stream in the quiet of the afternoon, she recalled how she had felt in this season the previous year. Still with her family in her protected forest home, she had begun to feel restless. She had taken short forays outside her family's territory, testing her courage, but had returned each time to the comfort and safety of her family's presence.

After several forays had led her farther and farther from home, she faced her mother, who looked into her eyes. Coyote's mother knew that soon her daughter would leave and that they would never see each other again. She knew her daughter's journey would challenge all her courage, but she also knew her daughter was ready and that it was time for her to leave. She had given her daughter all she needed to survive—all the skills, all the wariness, all that was coyote. Soon, when the time was right, Coyote would leave and never return.

Coyote's mate stared at her as she recalled that time, knowing her thoughts and feelings. He understood, for he too had become restless at this time the previous year. He too had tested himself, first on short and then on longer and longer forays away from his family. His mother, too, had looked at him with understanding but also concern, for she knew the dangers he would encounter. It was important that her son test himself and be ready to flee if necessary, for his parents' territory lay just on the edge of the protected forest, and they were exposed to danger every day as they hunted for food.

Coyote's mate painfully recalled that cold winter day

when both his parents were trapped and bludgeoned to death. He could still hear their cries of agony in the trap and their screams of terror as they were killed. His mother had known that this might come to pass, and she had wanted her son to be prepared to flee and to survive on his own. He did flee, and he did survive. But he had never had the chance to say goodbye to his parents as their bloodied bodies were dragged away.

Coyote and her mate had survived. They had undertaken perilous journeys, as their ancestors had been doing for thousands upon thousands of years. They had found each other, and they had found a new home. Resting on the riverbank, they understood that winter winds would soon be approaching, bringing hardships of hunger and cold. They looked knowingly at each other as they snuggled together and delighted in these fleeting moments of comfort. They would survive.

All life in the forest understood the message of the changes in the air and the shortening days. Squirrels were busy caching the many acorns that had fallen to the forest floor from the heights of the great oaks. Their lives were a balancing act. They needed to store as many acorns as possible before the snows came, but at the same time, they needed to be wary of the many hungry predators wanting to make a meal of them, especially those ever-present pine martins. Black bears were fattening themselves for their upcoming hibernations, that remarkable evolutionary process of slowing down everything in their bodies. They needed enough food to survive the winter.

The many songbirds who had serenaded Coyote and her mate through the summer were heading south in long migratory flights, taking their grown chicks and showing them the way. The swallows had completed their summer's insect patrol and, with winter approaching, would head far to the south and continue their work where the season was turning to summer again. But crow and raven would remain in the North Woods to keep Coyote and her mate company, sending them alerts of danger or potential food. And the remarkable chickadees, so tiny yet hearty, would continue to sing their chick-a-dee-dee-dee song into the winter, reminding all that spring would come again.

The bull moose were in rut, and the crashing of their antlers echoed from one mountain slope to another. Often, as Coyote and her mate were busy mousing or cornering a rabbit, the intense focus of their hunt was interrupted by the mating activity of the bull moose or the honking calls of Canada geese as they passed overhead in chevrons on their ancient migratory flight south.

This was the time of year their parents had warned them of over and over again—the time when traps were set by humans. Somehow, they both felt that they were safe in this place, for the humans they had observed here so far had not come to kill them. Despite that feeling, however, they would use great caution and their keen sense of smell to pick up the scent of any human.

Though all the life of the forest was preparing for winter, humans continued to visit the coyotes' territory, but still they were not carrying traps or guns or bringing dogs. And the humans never stayed, but soon left again. As the days became shorter and shorter and the nights colder, fewer and fewer humans could be heard or observed.

One evening just after sunset, Coyote and her mate caught a beaver foraging on the shore near his dam, and quickly ended his life. As they shared the body, they looked up to see the first snowflakes of winter beginning to fall in a soft veil of white. The mountaintops had been covered by snow since mid-autumn, and now the entire landscape would be blanketed in the majesty and harsh beauty of winter. The soft snowflakes soon turned into a curtain of white and continued to fall into the night. They cuddled under a great spruce, tucked their noses in their tails, and fell asleep with snow crystals falling gently on their thick golden fur. Later that night the snow ended and the clouds moved east, pushed by the westerly winds behind them. The light from a waxing moon created a sparkling landscape of tiny diamonds on the snow-covered earth. All was silent and still.

They awoke in the hushed morning twilight, covered by a blanket of glistening white. Looking at each other with glowing eyes, they stood up and shook the snow from their coats, sending it whirling about them in a wild frenzy. The new-fallen snow invited them to play. Down went their noses into the soft powder, and they happily tunneled wherever their noses felt like going. They described crazy circles, snow almost covering their faces, then both jumped up as if on cue and began to chase each other through the forest in glee. First she would chase him as he raced past trees and boulders and jumped over fallen branches, and then the tables would turn as he spun about and chased her in merry pursuit. Soon, however, he began to falter as his wounded leg felt the pain of cold.

They settled down together, and Coyote licked her mate's leg over and over again to warm and soothe it, understanding his pain. She would let him rest now and go off to hunt for both of them. Water was still flowing near the streams and wetlands, and mice and voles were sure to be found there. The rodents were well hidden under the new mantle of more than four inches of snow, but Coyote could always find them. Having procured morning food for herself and her mate, she was on her way back to him when she heard a swish, swish, swish and at the same moment smelled and saw a human.

Coyote stood motionless, a stiff statue of stillness. The human saw her, and their eyes met. They were traveling the same trail, but in opposite directions. She had been so intent on getting back to her mate that she had dropped her guard.

Coyote and the human looked at each other. After

a long moment the woman said, "You are safe here. We will stand up for you." Coyote did not understand the woman's words, but she felt the woman's compassion, and she understood. Still, she needed to keep her distance, so she retreated hurriedly into the forest. As she trotted away from the woman, Coyote turned again and again until the woman was no longer to be seen. The woman did not move. She stood in silence, feeling gratitude that she had been granted this momentary meeting with a beautiful wild being.

On her way back to her mate, Coyote recalled that she had seen that woman many times throughout the summer and autumn, and thought that maybe the woman was somehow watching over this place.

As she approached her mate, he trotted to her, licking her face and placing his paw over her neck. They had become inseparable now, and each return from an absence, no matter how brief, occasioned a joyful and affectionate greeting. She offered him the rodents she had been carrying in her stomach, and sat beside him as he consumed them. Later that morning, they would need to hunt again.

Raven came to their aid. He began croaking loudly from the branches of a spruce beside a small brook that entered the great wild stream they so enjoyed. Off they trotted to see what raven had discovered for them, and they saw a large old raccoon who appeared to be injured, as he was dragging one of his back legs. He would not make it through the winter.

Injured or not, a raccoon can be a formidable animal and must not be taken lightly. They knew they would need a trickster plot so their kill would be swift and safe. She would approach the raccoon from the front, distracting and effectively cornering him, while her mate would come from behind and clamp his canines and strong jaws around the prey's neck, instantly cutting off his breathing.

It could be a dangerous affair, for the raccoon might turn and give severe bites to Coyote's mate. But they plotted their combined actions and were swift and powerful in carrying them out. It is their wit that makes coyotes formidable predators. Native Peoples recognized, admired, and imitated coyotes in their own hunting.

Raccoons are not a favored prey of coyotes, but this was a meal that Coyote and her mate needed, and they would take advantage of any opportunity for survival as winter approached. But they did not forget to share with raven, who, throughout the millennia, had been their hunting companion. They left some for him to finish off.

The landscape was being transformed into a place of magnificent but fearsome beauty. The streams and ponds began to freeze, delicate ice crystals appearing each day and becoming something even more wonderful the next night. All appeared silent and still, but life was recreating itself within this landscape of snow and ice. Brutal north winds brought ever colder temperatures, testing the survival skills of all living beings in the forest. The great spruce, fir, and pines stood as tall sentinels, protecting those who sought shelter beneath their limbs, covered with sweet-smelling needles and dusted with new-fallen snow. The small mammals of the forest sought refuge deep underground or in the crevices between the many great, granite boulders strewn on the forest floor, remnants of the last great glacial period.

Hunting became more and more challenging for Coyote and her mate. There were days of lying still, waiting for a hare to emerge from its burrow or listening for the sound of mice running through their snowy tunnels beneath the snow. Each animal had learned its own means of survival; none would be caught unaware. Many a day brought nothing but hunger. Survival for a carnivore in the north woods in winter requires intelligence and savvy, force of will, and daily measures. Starvation ends the lives of many carnivores.

Coyote and her mate knew that death would stalk weak, old, starving, and injured animals in the time of bitter cold. Over and over again, raven or crow alerted them that another animal was approaching death. There is no waste in the winter forest; the death of one means continued life for another.

And this time of cold brought the promise of new life as well. One morning, Coyote went off in one direction to hunt for mice in the deep snow while her mate went in another, the two of them hoping to increase their success by hunting separately. But coyotes are always together even when far apart, for their connections are deep and lasting. Only they know how. Coyote and her mate had been hunting independently for two hours when she felt the need to let him know where she was. She threw her head back and howled from deep inside herself, and what she howled was a longing to be with him.

She had begun to feel a powerful urge within, the urge to mate with her life companion. Her body was changing, and her hormones were preparing her for motherhood. She knew that the time she was given by nature to become pregnant was short—only these few weeks, no more. The previous year she had been alone, and mating had been impossible.

She had hardly ended her song when she saw him trotting toward her with the unique gait created by the loss of his paw. His face was intent and focused on her in a way she had never seen before.

They had become profoundly close in their year together, reading each other's thoughts and feelings, understanding each other's pain and hunger. They had found joy in one another, each delighting in the other's company. They played together, swam and ran together, hunted together, ate together, sang to the moon and stars together, and slept together always. He understood that her time was at hand, and he felt it in his body as well. His coyote sense picked it up in the smell of her fur, the whiff of her breath, and the spot where she had just marked her territory.

He came to her and snuggled next to her, placing his paw on her shoulder and his head around her neck. And there in the snow-laden forest of a sunny, bitterly cold afternoon, their bodies became one, and they created new life, the first coyote life to be created in Maine. It was a historic moment for their kind, but the world knew nothing of it, and it was better so.

From that day they never left each other's presence. They were always together, trotting side by side or curled up close as they slept. She felt life inside her body. She remembered watching her mother hunt while pregnant with Coyote's younger brothers and sisters, at the same time teaching Coyote and her littermates winter hunting skills. Coyote's mother had been strong, courageous, and deeply bonded with Coyote's father, who watched over his mate with great care. They lived in wild canine mode—coyote and wolf mode—always counting on each other for their mutual survival and the survival of their pups. It would be so for Coyote and her mate as well; they would survive this winter together.

Nighttime temperatures were often dropping to the single digits or below zero, and the snowpack was increasing with every new storm. Often they would see heavy, dark gray-blue clouds massing over the mountains, a warning of yet another storm coming. Moving through the deep drifts built by the fierce winds forced them to employ all their energy reserves, which then had to be replaced with sustenance. As much as possible, they traveled under the great spruce, fir, and pine, whose limbs and needles kept much of the snow from the forest floor beneath them. Many days they did not attempt to travel or hunt, but reserved their energy and went without food.

As the snow grew deeper, moose moved slowly about in regenerating forest stands, seeking sustenance from twigs of willow, aspen, birch, and maple or branches of balsam fir. When the drifts were deepest, Coyote saw moose head toward higher elevations on the windswept mountains, where it was easier to travel and find sustenance. Though their metabolism slowed in the winter and allowed them to survive on stored fat, spring would inevitably find moose lying on trails, their famished bodies unable to go any farther.

Deer struggled to stay alive as well. Maine's north woods marked the northern limit of their range, and their numbers were low to begin with; harsh winters often caused death by starvation for many. They would seek out stands of spruce, fir, and pine that provided forage and created a canopy of protection from the elements. Coyote and her mate knew well where those wintering grounds were located in the sheltered valleys of their territory.

When it seemed that winter would never end, the days grew perceptibly longer and the midday sun conveyed just a bit of warmth into their fur coats. One morning after almost seven days without food, Coyote and her mate were struggling through the snow near an ice-covered pond. They desperately needed to find food that day, for they were weak and losing weight, and Coyote was pregnant with their pups. Very quietly, they came upon a group of deer standing stoically in their wintering ground. One elderly doe was lying down, too weak to rise when the rest of the small herd became alert to the coyotes' presence. The others bunched together and moved to a safer distance, leaving the old deer struggling to rise; but she could not.

This deer's impending death represented the coyotes' chance for survival. As they approached from behind to protect themselves from her hooves, she watched wide eyed and thrashed about, unable to defend herself. Coyote's mate sank his sharp canines deep into the doe's neck, cutting off her breathing and ending her suffering. She did not die a slow, ignominious death from starvation. The small herd stood at a distance, understanding that they were safe now. One of their kind had given her life so the rest could live.

Through her death, this aged deer would support many lives. As Coyote and her mate opened the deer's body to feed ravenously on her flesh, raven croaked his signal from a tall spruce overhead, then swooped to the ground with his mate. While the coyotes ate, the ravens strutted about. Soon their yearling chicks arrived, summoned by their parents' call, and joined the restless waiting, for they knew the coyotes would save food for them. It was an ancient pact, this sharing.

After they had eaten all they were able, Coyote and her mate trotted over to a great pine, settled down under it, and rested. They would return the next day and eat their fill again. In the winter, each meal was a matter of survival. Now it was the ravens' turn.

Later that day, in midafternoon, Coyote and her mate awoke to the swish, swish, swish sound of snowshoes on a nearby path. They remained still as two statues snuggled together, neither making a movement. Their eyes met the eyes of the woman again as she stopped and recognized them through the forest cover. After a moment she said, "I see you have a mate, and I see you know how to survive." She looked at the partially eaten body of the old deer. "She was an old one, I can tell," the woman observed. "I am glad you are here."

Not wanting to leave their cherished food too far behind, they retreated a short distance into the forest and sat on their haunches. They understood that they were safe with her, but their true wildness urged them always to keep a safe distance. The woman, understanding, left them. Again she spoke softly as her snowshoes tracked through the snow, "You are safe here." Coyote looked at her mate, communicating to him in their silent language that this was the woman she had seen before. She did not know what the woman was saying, but she sensed what the woman was thinking and feeling. Coyote sensed that her pups could safely share the world with people like this. Her innate wildness knew this but could not speak it out loud.

9

March through June 1971

The light began to soften as the days grew longer and the sun climbed higher in the sky. Temperatures no longer dropped to the single digits at night. Winter's hard-edged clarity and severe beauty gave way, bit by bit, to the milder air of early spring. The time of new life in the forest was approaching, and so was the birth of Coyote's pups.

She was midway through her pregnancy and could feel her little ones in her body. They were infused with coyote genes from their parents' mothers and with wolf genes from their parents' fathers. Now both species would carry on through Coyote, a testimonial to the ongoing wonder of evolution, which continues to bring forth the finest and strongest of nature's manifestations.

It was time to move to a safe refuge for the birth of the pups, a place Coyote and her mate had scouted as they had explored and marked their territory. One morning when fluffy clouds were chasing each other eastward across soft blue skies, the two of them traveled together through the slowly melting snow to their chosen den site in an area that was remote from human trails and near many small streams that tumbled down from the mountains. Coyote would dig her den on a ledge between two giant granite boulders that would protect it from the rain and cold of early spring. The nearby stream banks harbored the rodents she and her mate would need to feed themselves and, later, their growing pups.

The snow in the valleys was giving way to the sun's warmth, and the ice on the lakes was breaking up, creaking and crackling as great chunks slid over and under one another and huge cracks split, exposing the watery depths once more. Streams were breaking out of winter's icy hold and burgeoning into wild and raging waters as mountain snows melted and found their way down to the valleys below. Coyote would dig her den facing south, so that the sun would warm the nursery. She began the ancient tradition of her kind. She alone would dig the den, while her mate set out to hunt for both of them.

She had watched her mother prepare a den for her younger siblings. This was a very personal act of motherhood prompted by the heartbeat of the little ones within. And now Coyote was creating a den for her own first litter of pups. She was intent and focused on this labor of motherhood; it had to be perfect, it had to be safe.

Her mate understood his role as the birth of their

pups approached. He became a superb hunter, for his coyote spirit found ways to compensate for his wounded leg. At times Coyote would hunt with her mate, hunger taking her away from her den preparation for a time. But when she was meticulously digging her den, he would return and lay a rabbit down for her to eat. He had learned the secret to catching a snowshoe hare; he needed to ambush it, not attempt to chase it as the lynx was able. He would set out just before dawn to sit and wait for the hare returning to its burrow, and catch it unaware.

Sometimes he did not need to hunt, for the winter had taken many lives by starvation. He discovered another dying deer with the assistance of raven's call. The yearling deer was so weak it could not rise, and his back leg was broken, with blood seeping from the shattered bone that had pierced the flesh. The deer could do nothing but accept his fate stoically as Coyote's mate approached. In one swift act of nature's mercy, her mate ended the yearling's life. In death, as in life, this young deer remained an integral part of life in the forest.

Nourished through her mate's splendid hunting skills, Coyote was free to prepare her den. Her mate would return from hunting to a barrage of dirt and pebbles flying out from underneath her body, her front paws working tirelessly to dig and sling debris with astonishing velocity. At first when he returned, he would see her pelvis and tail, then he would see only her tail, and finally he saw only dirt and pebbles flying out as her den grew deeper and deeper in the earth. She always sensed when he returned and immediately backed up out of her den to greet him. Her beautiful face was covered with earth. She had a gleam in her eye and a grin on her face for him. They danced about on the melting snow, happy in each other's company and anticipating the birth of their pups. More and larger sunny patches of forest floor emerged, freed from the weight of deep snow and offering the promise of new life ready to burst forth in freedom.

They would rest together, he placing his nose on her abdomen and gently nuzzling it there as though communicating with his unborn pups. He was going to be a father soon, and in coyotes' highly sophisticated social lives, fatherhood is of immense importance. Within days, he would be the sole provider of food for both himself and his mate. She would depend completely on him for sustenance from the day she withdrew into her den to give birth to the day, many days later, when she emerged. He would also be her protector, standing guard at the den whenever he was not hunting.

They both understood the immense courage and self-reliance it would take to raise their pups without the help of an extended family, for they had both experienced in youth how vital all the members of the family were. With older siblings to guard the den, hunt for food, and later to play with the pups, the pups need never be left alone even in the den. The den was not always safe, for potential predators could easily get whiffs of the new life underground and vehemently dig to find and kill them.

Coyote had one more den to dig before her pups were born. Always, always there needed to be an escape den to which they could flee to keep their pups safe if a predator discovered them. If the den of their birth became infested with fleas or ticks, she had to have another den ready for her pups, for these parasites could kill her little ones if left to multiply and invade their tiny bodies. Her den was to be kept a secret from all others. She chose another safe location on a ledge made from granite boulders. It was a distance away, but close enough for adequate food and easy escape.

Then her time arrived. She had gone to the stream to drink its refreshing waters and then waited for her mate's return. He knew it was her time as well, for they were on this journey of new parenthood together. On his return, he offered her numerous rodents he had held in his stomach, then stood over her as she ate. Each licked the other's muzzle and leaned into the fur of the other's neck, remaining there for a few quiet moments of intimacy; then she turned and entered her den while he watched her disappear.

Coyote was entering a new world, that of motherhood. She was four years old, and she was ready, but it is a momentous challenge to become a wild mother. She was well aware of the dangerous world into which she was bringing her small pups. Without the customary extended family of coyote culture, everything depended on her and her mate.

Once she found her way through the snug entrance of the den and maneuvered her way several feet into the nursery she had created, she lay down and gently plucked some fur from her abdomen. It would be the bedding on which her pups would rest after they were born. The freshly dug earth of her den was pungent with the sweet smell of the forest soil, and its fragrance encompassed her as she lay within its protection. She rested quietly, waiting for her body to bring forth her little ones. Ever since she had met her mate, they had experienced everything together, but the birth of her pups was something she must do alone. The wisdom of her body and her ancient knowledge of how to respond to that wisdom was within her.

The moment came when she felt the powerful push of her body to release her first pup. The little one came forth softly, and she immediately attended to him, assisting him out from his placental covering and licking him all over with her warm tongue. He was tiny and helpless; his eyes were closed, and his little legs thrashed about gently as she tucked him under her warm coat of fur. And then her next pup came forth, and the next, and the next—four in all. She cared gently for each one and ate the placental remains. Now all four pups were whimpering, straining their little bodies to seek their mother's milk. She tucked them all in her embrace and allowed them to nurse until they fell asleep. She had given birth for the first time, and the experience of bringing forth these precious little lives consumed her. Now she would rest with them.

Meanwhile outside the den, her mate paced with excitement, for he knew his little pups had been born. She had spoken to him through an intimate, soft song before she rested with her little ones. Now he must announce their birth to the forest, the mountains, the sky, and all life that had ears to hear. Dancing about in a tight circle, he threw his head high, facing the sunny blue sky of this beautiful day, and howled his coyote song of joy. This was a whole new experience in their lives. There was such excitement over these perfect little pups they had brought into the world, but with it came the immense responsibility of parenthood. As Coyote's mate paced back and forth in front of the den, both of these emotions came to him. He knew the life of a wild canine. He knew all the happiness they were capable of experiencing, but he also knew the hardships and dangers, the pain and suffering. He would give himself entirely to fatherhood and seek relentlessly to nourish and protect the pups and their mother.

They had experienced this day of wonder together though apart. In the early evening, however, he had to leave her for a while to hunt for both of them. He left with great reservation, letting her know that he would be gone for a short while. As he trotted off, he kept looking back at the den until it was out of sight. He was intensely aware that he was leaving the den unguarded, and he knew too well the danger that entailed. He and his mate were pioneers in a new landscape, alone with their pups.

Quietly approaching a snowshoe hare burrow he had scouted previously, he sat motionless, waiting for the hare to emerge on his evening excursion. His timing was right. Out stepped the hare, and before the swift animal could speed away, the coyote secured him around the neck and ended his life immediately.

Just then his keen ears heard two hikers talking on a trail a long distance away. He sensed a third human there, too, the woman the coyotes had seen several times before. On this day she had been photographing early signs of life returning to the park when the two hikers approached. One said, "Caroline, I see your name on your badge. You're the ranger's wife, yes? We thought we heard howling a good distance away from here. It sounded really excited. What was that?"

Caroline said nothing for a moment, because she was most cautious about sharing the coyotes' presence in the park. Then she answered, "We have coyotes living in the park. They like to howl." Wide-eyed, the hikers answered, "Ohhh, ohhh, okay. . . ." They went on their way, wondering, and the woman went on hers. By then Coyote's mate had taken off toward the den with the hare in his mouth, food for his mate.

Approaching the den, he sniffed its immediate vicinity, confirming for himself that no threat had approached while he was gone. Satisfied that all was safe, he whined softly to let her know that he had returned with food. She emerged slowly, licked his muzzle, and retreated with the hare. Ravenous, she consumed every bit of it, leaving only a few large bones behind, for her body now needed more sustenance than ever in order to feed her pups. Rearranging herself within the tight den, she tucked her sleeping little ones under her warm fur, and they all went to sleep.

Her mate needed to hunt for himself now, but he did not go far. He plucked many a rodent from vanishing tunnels beneath the melting snow along nearby stream banks, then quickly returned to the den. Curling up at the entrance, which was hidden by a large spruce, he slept in fits and starts. That night the cold rains of early spring came. All night it rained, saturating the landscape and his fur, but he did not move. He remained on guard through the night.

The skies cleared in the early morning. The night's rain had washed the landscape of its remaining vestiges of wet snow, exposing new sprouts of life to respond to spring sunshine. Coyote's mate awoke to the honking of Canada geese that were flying overhead on their way north. Their great spring migration was taking them home for the birth of their chicks. Songbirds, too, were returning once more from their epic migrations and filling the treetops with mating songs. New life was pouring forth everywhere around the coyotes' nursery, and the parents of all newborns would be tirelessly seeking food for them.

Hunting for food was the focus of Coyote's mate now. In a whirlwind of canine shaking, he let loose the wet layer of rain from his fur, reenergized himself with a long, slow canine stretch, and walked to the entrance of the den. He could hear his little ones making soft puppy sounds and his mate rearranging her body to nurse them. Whimpering to let her know that he was leaving, he took off to find food for her, returning an hour later with a stomach full of mice that she quickly consumed.

Their little ones remained in their den nursery until late spring, sleeping and then whimpering when hungry for their mother's milk. Coyote gently cleaned them over and over again with her warm tongue and tucked them within her thick fur to protect them from the cold. This was a most intimate time; her whole being was centered on her beguiling pups. Each day they became more active, crawling about on their tiny legs and bumping into and rolling over each other as their mother carefully observed their newborn antics. Innocent of the world into which they had been born, they gave themselves entirely to the present moments of comfort. Outside the den, Coyote's mate hunted food as close by as he was able, and otherwise stood guard faithfully or slept outside the den entrance. He was on high alert.

Two weeks went by, and as Coyote lay curled with her pups, a thrilling moment occurred. Their blue eyes had opened, and when a shaft of light found its way down into the den, they saw their mother for the first time. She stared at them, gazing into their innocent blue eyes and knowing the intelligence expressed there, an intelligence that would guide them through their lives. A whole new world of discovery began for the pups; a world of communing with each other and their environment. Not long after, Coyote began to notice that she was feeling their little emerging teeth nipping her from time to time as they nursed. Her pups were growing and changing almost daily under the solicitous care of their parents.

Danger existed in many forms, one of which was always potentially present within the den itself—ticks and fleas. She noticed these invading parasites crawling about the den, and began to carefully check her pups, not allowing the insects to become embedded in their tender skin. These parasites were capable of inflicting great harm on her little ones. Her maternal instinct would tell her when to leave the den, and these parasites would soon force her to make the move.

One evening when her mate returned from his hunting, he stopped suddenly as he approached the den. A female bear with her newborn cub was attempting to plow her way into the den. He would not have it. He had to keep himself safe because he knew his mate needed him to survive, but he must protect the den at all costs.

Growling, he charged the cub at high speed, knocking him down and causing him to run off, squealing in terror. The mother bear reeled and reared to her hind legs, threatening him with her sharp claws, but he would not back down. Ears back, mouth agape, he snarled and bared his canines. The bear dropped to four legs and lunged with seemingly impossible speed for such a bulky animal, but he was coyote and he was even faster, even with an injured leg. Moving with lightning speed to her rear, he plunged his canines into her back before she could swing around.

The next moment could have been the last for Coyote's mate, but the bear's cub was bleating, and the call of motherhood was more powerful than the urge to challenge this fiercely determined coyote. Growling, the bear took off in the direction of her young one, giving her combatant one more threatening look over her shoulder.

Exhausted and shaken, Coyote's mate collapsed at the door of the den and whined to her, wanting to know if Coyote and the little ones were safe. She softly whined back, letting him know that they were. When she knew it was safe to emerge, she received the food from his evening hunt, nestled with him, then returned to feed her whimpering pups. Despite his exhaustion, he stood guard on high alert in the event that the bear should return.

Given the bear attack and the beginning of a tick and flea infestation, Coyote and her mate knew it was time to move their pups to the other den she had prepared. Several hours later, when they were quite sure the bear and her cub were gone, Coyote emerged from her den with a pup in her mouth. She paused there, allowing her mate to see his little one for the first time and to gently lick the little dangling body, then she trotted off with the pup while her mate guarded the den. Back and forth she went with the second, third, and fourth pups, and her mate greeted each one with a warm lick on the small body dangling from her mouth. When she carried her last little one to their new den, he followed intently. As he stood guard, she ran back to the old den and checked it one more time to make sure all her pups were gone. There could be no miscalculations, because in the wild, there is rarely a second chance.

Spring had definitely arrived, for the black flies hatched on schedule. Five weeks after the birth of the pups and two weeks after they had been moved to the new den, a most exciting but frightening moment arrived for Coyote and her mate. At their bidding, their pups emerged from the den for the first time. While their four little ones scrambled up out of the den with ears cocked to their parents' encouraging calls and bright little eyes squinting in the sunshine, Coyote recalled a similar moment in her own life four years before. The time of newborn intimacy was over. As their small faces greeted the world they would inhabit, her pups began the most dangerous time of their lives.

10

June to October 1971

Coyote remembered how she and her littermates had first tumbled out of their den, not quite knowing what to do with their little legs, excited in their freedom and falling on top of each other. Now she was the mother, and she watched with pleasure as her little ones discovered the outside world for the first time. Her mate remained close to the pups, affectionately licking them one at a time, creating that close bond of fatherhood that is essential to coyote culture. Both parents hovered over the pups, keeping them close to the entrance. Within this protective circle of utmost solicitude, the little ones tested their unsteady legs, racing after each other, pouncing on siblings in a game of surprise, and falling into happy heaps. They were fascinated by each other's tails and would find every chance to tug them.

All this activity soon sent them to Coyote to nurse. They stretched up on their little back legs to reach her while she stood guard, ready at any time to hustle the pups into the den should she or her mate detect danger. With their stomachs full of their mother's milk, the pups settled into a nap in the sunshine, piling up and cuddling each other in innocent sleep. When the sun sank in the west, their parents herded them back into the den.

This exciting introduction to their world was the beginning of a complex, imperative instructional endeavor. The pups needed to learn all the skills necessary to hunt effectively in any season. They needed to learn how to find food and detect the smell of prey. They needed to know their prey's hiding places and comings and goings, when to seek them, and how to catch them.

They needed to learn everything about their parents' territory—the trees of the forest, the streams and lakes, the shapes of the mountains towering over the valleys, the bushes where berries could be found, the rocks and boulders that served as signposts or lookouts. They needed to learn about other predators that moved through the landscape and how to behave with them, and they needed to learn about humans. They needed to learn how to survive.

The first step in this course of instruction was to introduce the pups to the smell, taste, and texture of what would be their primary food throughout life—rodents. The siblings would be weaned within a couple weeks, and from that time forward would need ever-growing amounts of food. One of the pups, much smaller than the other three, concerned her parents. She seemed vibrant and playful, but she was so small. They hoped she would catch up with her siblings once she began eating solid food.

The next day Coyote's mate set out to hunt not only for Coyote, but also for their pups. He returned an hour later with two squirrels in his mouth, both for her. These small mammals of the treetops had been so busy finding fresh spring food for themselves that he had taken them by surprise on the ground after sitting silently and watching their activity. Coyote hastily consumed both squirrels as her mate took off to find mice for the pups.

Late in the afternoon, he returned with a stomach full of rodents. After a quick inspection of the vicinity of the den, he whimpered and she promptly emerged with a smile on her face, her whole body wiggling in giddy exuberance, her tail wildly swinging about. She ran around him in an excited dance and nuzzled up to him with affection.

She was followed by her pups, who sought out their father for his greeting and then straight away began attempting to stand over each other and initiate puppy wrestling, their means of establishing dominance among themselves. Both parents immediately recognized that one female pup had become the most dominant, and their very small female pup was the least dominant of the four. Once the pups had established each other's rank that day, they went into full-fledged play, tumbling happily about under their parents' watchful eyes.

Before they could approach their mother to nurse, however, their father intercepted them and brought forth from his stomach four predigested mice. They stopped, sniffed this strange food, and stared up at their parents, who were communicating to them in a language only coyotes know: *This is food for you.* At that, the dominant female pup approached the strange food, licked it, and slowly began to consume it. Her littermates followed suit, the small female pup having her fill as well. Then they approached their mother to nurse, after which the whole family curled up to rest, the little ones snuggling in their parents' warm embrace.

At dusk, Coyote escorted the pups back into the den. Before following them, she approached her mate and they silently shared the pleasure of having successfully introduced their little ones to wild food. The pups would need to learn much in order to survive as wild carnivores. Step by step, their parents would teach them.

Night fell, but the forest is never asleep. There was always the crackling of small branches in the underbrush close by or the splashing of unknown footsteps through nearby brooks. In contrast, there was the silence of the great horned owl's wings as it swooped down on unsuspecting prey. In the forest during the spring, all life is hungry and searching for food day and night. Her mate would sleep with all senses on high alert.

Once darkness hid her presence, the lynx began her

nightly search for food for her young. She slipped by Coyote's mate, who smelled her presence and, with a coyote's awareness, felt her large paws moving cautiously past him at a distance. They paid each other no heed as she slipped into the brush. The lynx had to feed her kittens, too.

Each day brought the pups into the world outside their den once more, and each day they discovered more about the agility of their bodies and the acuteness of their senses as they played and romped. They would discover a tiny branch to call their own, and sink their small teeth into it, or claim a rock to rest on and then leap upon one of their brothers or sisters, or peek inside a large limb that had fallen to the ground. Everything that moved or made the slightest sound or song caught their attention. They cocked their heads when they heard songbirds in the treetops above them or the scramble of a red squirrel fleeing a pine martin.

All sorts of scents emanated from the forest floor and beneath it, and their noses followed intently to discover where each one came from. They experienced the warmth of sunny blue skies and gazed in wonder at clear nights studded with innumerable stars, the moon a shining sliver of white. On one of those nights they saw their parents throw their heads back in delight and sing with coyote yips and yaps, yips and yaps. They could not contain themselves, and out of their tiny mouths held high to the night sky, the pups squealed their own first happy yips and yaps into that place between ordinary reality and fantasy where true life dwells, that place of wonder, delight, and awe.

The pups continued to investigate every new insect they observed crawling on the forest floor or slithering under the leaf litter, following with intent eyes and flicking paws. They pounced on jumping grasshoppers and, to their supreme surprise, captured them. In their play they were honing their skills of observation and focused attention, and little by little they became aware of the capabilities of their paws and teeth. But when they heard the raven's call in the spruce tree overhead, they scampered under the safety of their mother or father. Somehow, they seemed to know about the raven's call. Every day brought new adventures, but only under the watchful eyes of their parents, who kept the pups in close proximity to the den at all times.

There were days when Coyote's mate was away hunting and she wanted to know where he was, and if he was safe. As she lifted her head to howl for him, her little ones gathered and lifted their tiny faces to the sky, mimicking their mother, letting out their excited yips and yaps that continued to sound more like squeaking yelps. Their excitement grew when their father responded from afar. They were beginning to recognize that they could communicate with each other even when they were apart, and they were beginning to learn coyote language, the intricate and sophisticated communication that only they understand. Their singing did not go unnoticed by the park's numerous human visitors that summer, who, upon hearing the songs, tried to imagine the beings capable of such a wide range of astonishing vocalizations.

The pups' growing bodies began to change conspicuously. As newborns they had sported soft, dark-brown fur coats, but in time their coats thickened and turned a golden tone. Their tails grew bushier, and each one kept a black tail tip—a coyote signature! Their legs grew longer, and their ears looked way too big for the little faces that were beginning to sprout a coyote's long muzzle. Coyote and her mate recognized each one of their four pups not only by their unique personalities—which were evident early on—but also by each one's signature look—slight touches of white or dark brown or tan that only their parents would recognize.

With summer in full sway, deerflies hatched in merciless numbers. Human hikers also came in greater numbers to the park, often hiking into remote areas closer to where Coyote and her mate were caring for their pups. She had weaned them from nursing, and they were thriving on the mice their father and mother caught for them. For all these reasons, it was time for the pups to abandon their den for good and follow their parents wherever they traveled. In the twilight of a warm summer day, Coyote and her mate guided the little ones away from the den and, with concerned solicitude, traveled deeper into the remote areas of their territory. They would choose rendezvous sites where the pups could rest and hide while awaiting the return of their parents from hunting trips too arduous for them.

In valleys overshadowed by the towering mountains, small brooks tumbled toward larger streams that, in time, received other brooks and swelled into still larger streams, supporting the vibrant life that throbbed through this rich landscape. Coyote and her mate guided their pups to these places of abundance. They wanted to remain close to the streams, where numerous rodents and refuge from the biting insects and heat of summer could be found.

Now came the constant challenge of keeping the little ones together. Each distracting new experience sent their curious minds wandering: a flying insect or butterfly, a swish in the branches of a young spruce, the scent of a skunk or raccoon that had passed that way during the night. Their senses were thrilled by the new world into which their parents were leading them. The family traveled slowly, allowing the little ones to play on the journey. Within the hour, they needed a nap. Coyote tucked them in a safe, shady space and rested with them while their father took off to hunt for the family. These rendezvous sites were now their places of safekeeping.

Within an hour he returned, holding a small mouse in his mouth. Up shot the pups, in great excitement at their father's return. Their first official hunting lesson was about to begin. Coyote positioned them in a small circle, and then, while she looked on, their father placed the mouse in the circle.

At first the frightened creature sat motionless, but soon it began to move, at which point one of the male pups pounced on it and held it with his forepaws, not quite knowing what to do next. Given this opportunity to escape, the mouse freed itself from the pup's grasp and began to run. Not to be left out, the small female pup aggressively blocked the mouse, holding it closely in her paw. She looked questioningly at her parents, soliciting them in wordless coyote language: *Now what do I do?* Her father let her know that she should bite the mouse and eat it, and somehow she understood. Quickly she ended the mouse's life and enjoyed the first meal that she herself had caught.

Her two brothers and sister looked at her and understood. Now they wanted a chance. The family traveled to a nearby stream where their mother and father caught three more mice for them. Around and around the pups went, chasing the mice, sometimes flipping them into the air by accident as they landed on their backs while trying so hard to hold onto their prey. After much scuffling and scurrying about, their prizes were won and their first hunting lesson was complete.

They would need many more mice to eat, for they were growing quickly. Leaving them under their father's care, Coyote herself moved carefully along the stream banks in search of mice for herself and her pups. It was almost noon when she returned, having consumed her fill and saved many more for her little ones. As she approached, they ran happily to her, licking her mouth and asking for their next meal, and she spread it out before them.

Exploration and crucial new lessons kept the pups active all morning, but the forest warmed as midday approached, slowing the whole family down. Coyote and her mate, with their pups tucked between them, headed toward a nearby brook, planning a first lesson in coyote swimming before their afternoon nap. When the pups' little paws touched the cool water, they quickly stepped back, not knowing what to make of it. But then they saw their mother move to the center of the brook and sit down to rest.

Watching their parents always gave the pups confidence, so they tried again while their father stood over them, encouraging them gently. Cautiously they stepped forward into the edge of the brook—one of the male pups first, followed by his wary siblings. Soon they rushed their mother, who was awaiting their approach, and paddled around her, their inquisitive faces wide eyed and wondering. Their father stood close by, vigilant, while their caution erupted into excited puppy yipping. They pawed the pebbles they discovered beneath the clear water and splashed each other in happy frolicking.

Another lesson completed, the whole family splashed ashore, creating a whirlwind of water flying in all directions as they shook themselves dry. Worn out by the excitement, the pups curled themselves into a tight bundle of puppy fur, surrounded by their resting but ever-watchful parents. There in the shade of a protecting fir, they slept all afternoon.

Time soon slipped into mid-summer, and the pups grew faster every day, honing their hunting skills as they followed their parents and observed them intently. Coyote and her mate taught them the "silent wait"—that patient, quiet, absolutely still watching for the preoccupied hare or the distracted squirrel on which to pounce. All four pups would lie motionless as they watched her execute the hunting skill of ambush. They would need to watch their parents many times, then attempt it themselves and fail many times. In the warm summer evenings, fireflies flicked their little lights off and on as they flitted about in the forest. The eyes of the pups would follow the winking lights in wonder, and they would chase the lights and attempt to catch them with their paws, to no avail.

Often when naptime approached, the little female pup would climb on her father's back when he was resting, and sit there as if he were her pony. She so liked to be with him in this way. The two little male pups loved to roughhouse with their mother, tugging her tail and running in circles around her. She would respond in kind, sending them on a merry chase. The dominant female pup would often approach her father when the little female was sitting on his back, and she would tug his tail and want to wrestle with him. He patiently allowed both his daughters to communicate with him in their own way. Deep bonds of affection and loyalty grew within their family. The parents delighted in how each of their pups was thriving under their solicitous care.

In late summer, Coyote and her mate led their pups to a raspberry patch at the foot of a sun-soaked mountain, where they demonstrated how to pluck berries without letting thorns pierce their faces. This was another new adventure, and the pups darted about seeking all the berries they could reach. Thus they were introduced to these sweet delights of nature, which they would henceforth and for the rest of their lives seek out in season.

Then the family traveled to the blueberry barrens that Coyote and her mate had discovered the previous summer in the southern portion of their territory. There they taught the pups to pluck the succulent small fruits in mouthfuls, and their small faces turned bright with delight as their cheeks puffed out with the treasured treats. These were happy, carefree days in the pups' young lives.

As autumn approached, Coyote and her mate understood that they needed to allow their pups more independence to begin exploring the world on their own. They had not yet allowed the pups to travel far from them, keeping constant communication with them through their howling language. Knowing all the dangers of the wild, they hesitated to take the next leap, but the young ones were restless. They were four and a half months old now and had learned many survival skills from their parents. Reluctantly, their parents allowed the pups to venture into their territory without hovering over them.

A week after the pups were permitted to adventure on their own, the happy summer days ended abruptly for one. The whole family had dispersed to hunt in the early morning, and one of the male pups was happily plucking raspberries when he noticed movement just beyond the bushes. Coyotes have an immense desire to investigate anything new to them, and he could not resist squeezing his face into the bush to see who was responsible for that movement. In a flash, a porcupine thrust his quills into the pup's face and mouth. Screaming in pain, the pup fell back writhing on the ground. Hearing his cries, his parents rushed to him with his brother and sisters following close behind.

Coyote and her mate knew all too well the seriousness of this attack. Their three other pups huddled together, stretching their necks and trying to understand what had happened to their sibling. Seeing her little one in such agony was painful and frightening for Coyote, for she felt powerless to help him. As he writhed and screamed, she lay down next to him and attempted to pull out the quills from his face with her teeth, periodically licking the top of his head to comfort him. She was able to remove a number of them, but she could not get to any in his mouth or near his eyes, and there were still many embedded in his face that she could not pull out. Her mate hovered over her, keeping the other three pups close and not allowing them to stray.

Coyote looked up at her mate after attempting to remove the quills for more than an hour. She had removed all she could, but her little one continued to cry, thrashing his head and front paws about and attempting to free his face from the other quills—to no avail. It was late morning, and the day was warm. After much encouragement, she was able to help the pup rise and walk slowly next to her to the nearby stream. There she had him lie down and rinsed his face with the cool water, hoping to ease his pain and possibly release more quills, although her coyote knowledge told her this would not work. The family then moved under a great fir and remained in its cool shade for the afternoon. The wounded pup, exhausted by trauma and thrashing, fell into a restless sleep, and Coyote lay down next to him, her body embracing him. She was in deep sorrow.

Although the pups knew how to hunt for mice, on this evening they remained close to their mother. At dusk, her mate knew he needed to hunt for the entire family, and he left Coyote with the pups snuggling close to her. They were afraid, for they sensed their parents' concern for their brother, who whined with pain as he slipped in and out of sleep. Coyote attempted to comfort him and to give him courage by licking his forehead and holding him close.

Later that evening, her mate returned with a stomach full of mice and voles, which he spread before his little ones. They were ravenous and consumed the food immediately, but the injured male would not touch the food. Later that night, Coyote's mate returned with a hare for her and then regurgitated another few predigested mice for their male pup, but again he would not touch the food. It was a night of restlessness and deep sorrow.

For the next several days, she never left her little one's side. He continued to refuse all offerings of food, becoming weaker and weaker without food or water, and Coyote could smell a growing infection within his mouth. On the fifth day, she and her mate again carried him to the stream, where she swished cool water on his face and attempted to get some into his mouth. By this time, he had become almost unresponsive, whining for his mother and then falling into a semi-comatose state.

His brother and sisters were cared for by their father but kept coming back to their brother and nestling down next to him. Coyote never left his side. In the morning twilight of the seventh day, the pup left this world surrounded by his family and embraced by his mother. She was inconsolable. They buried him under the great fir tree, tucking him into a bed of needles. His short life was over.

The whole family sang their sorrow, expressing their loss to the mountains. Hearing them, the woman recognized a song of sorrow, not joy. She was coming to know some of the happenings of their lives through their songs.

That morning, Coyote left her three pups in the care of their father and went off alone for a day. Her mate understood what she needed to do. She traveled all around the great lake, releasing her sorrow and deep sense of loss. She settled under the forest cover along her favorite wild stream and remained there until dark. A burgeoning full moon shone onto her face, sustaining her as she lay there alone.

Coyote moved through her grief and returned to her mate and her three pups. They needed her. Motherhood in the wild does not allow an extended time to grieve, and she knew she must care for her remaining pups and comfort her mate, who also was grieving. To let them know she was returning, she raised her face to the night sky and howled her mourning call, and they responded with excited howling. As she trotted back to where they were resting, her surviving pups ran excitedly to her with big smiles on their faces and tails wagging wildly. Her mate approached and gently licked her muzzle, and she, his. They needed to go on, for the sake of their pups and themselves.

11

October 1971 to February 1972

The insects that had so harassed the coyote family during the time of heat and humidity were disappearing, especially the nasty deerflies that had attempted to burrow their fangs into the pups' delicate ears and caused painful swelling and inflammation. As the nights became cool and comfortable once more, the nagging mosquitoes ceased the irritating buzzing that had kept the family's ears flicking in sleep. Since their brother's death, the pups had become more wary, using greater caution when approaching anything new or detecting a hidden sound.

Observing this newfound caution, Coyote and her mate encouraged their pups to become more and more independent, honing their hunting skills and traveling independently through the special places in their territory that their parents had guided them to previously—high places that made excellent lookouts, the best fishing streams and ponds, raspberry and blueberry patches, hiding places of mice and voles, and trees that squirrels favored. They were even becoming adept at fishing for trout after many hours of watching their parents.

And they came to understand the changing of the seasons and the rituals of life in preparation for the coming time that would stretch the survival skills of all life in the north country. Their heads cocked in wonder when they witnessed migrating flocks of birds and ducks; they stood back and cautiously viewed the mating rituals of the bull moose; and they watched with curiosity the busy caching of winter food by small mammals. And then, one cold day when the temperature had plummeted, the pups noticed white wet crystals falling from the sky, some landing on their eyelashes or noses to their delight and excitement. It was snowing. Winter had arrived.

They were seven months old. Their fur coats had grown luxurious and thick, and they could hunt for themselves, but they had never experienced the challenges that this time of year would bring. They continued to remain under their parents' solicitous care, for there were many more lessons to learn about surviving a winter. Howling was their means of communicating with each other and a source of comfort as well. They knew where every member of the family was and if they were safe. They intimately knew each other's voices and what each was saying.

The days became shorter, and the midday sun sank toward the southern horizon. Coyote was making her territorial rounds one midafternoon, leaving her scat and scent-marking, when she heard a soft howl, or maybe a whine. Then she heard it again, more clearly, a whine full of panic, not threat. She approached closer, on high alert for danger, then heard it yet again. She raised her nose to catch the scent. It is coyote scent, she thought.

She saw blood on the snow, a trail of blood, and at the end of the trail lay a yearling coyote, eyes glazed in pain, with a mangled foreleg, her front left paw missing. She rolled onto her back, exposing her abdomen in submission, as Coyote approached her. In their unspoken communication, body language said all that was needed—the young female's act of submission and Coyote's eyes and gentle demeanor, expressing acceptance and concern.

Coyote could not leave the wounded one to fend for herself as winter approached. Where had she come from, and where and how had this grievous injury occurred? Coyote could not know that the yearling had dispersed from her family far to the west, just as Coyote herself had done almost two years before. The yearling had stayed clear of traps and snares through most of her long journey, but in her fatigue and hunger she had fallen victim to one of the traps that littered the landscape just west of the park. Like Coyote's mate, she too had paid a great price for her freedom with the loss of a paw.

Coyote must let her mate know, but first she

approached the wounded yearling and licked her muzzle in acceptance, then carefully cleansed her wound with her warm tongue. Then she called to her family. They responded within moments and were soon on their way to her. As they approached, her mate knew right away what had happened, for he saw before him a young coyote who was suffering what he had suffered. Their young ones again nestled together, frightened by the blood and suffering they saw before them. They stood motionless as their parents communicated with this new coyote.

She and her mate looked at each other and communicated in their silent language. They would adopt the yearling, and she would become a member of their extended family. This was not a new behavior in coyote culture, for coyotes live in many ways, doing whatever it takes to survive. Their territory was rich with food, and they knew there would be enough for all. The yearling was thin and weak, her wound still open and bleeding. Fearing to interrupt her journey to attend to her leg, she had pushed herself forward, beyond the limits of her endurance, despite her suffering.

The parents allowed their pups to approach her, and the yearling understood that these three young ones were their pups and precious to them. Though too young to understand the full import of this day's happening, the pups knew that their parents had welcomed the yearling into their family. She should not have to travel any farther; her leg needed to heal, and she needed to rest. They would help each other survive this winter.

The falling snow was creating a thin layer of white upon the landscape, and Coyote and her mate set out hunting together this time, while their pups remained close to the female yearling and hunted mice in the wetlands around a nearby pond. The parents had not traveled far when their keen noses detected something that caused them to move with great caution. Their searching eyes observed blood on the fresh snow, and they followed its trail to a hemlock grove and a deer whose face was covered with blood from a gunshot wound to her jaw. She was attempting to eat from the lower hemlock branches, but her jaw was shattered from the wound, and she could not. Stoic, she stood unsteadily, barely able to remain upright, pain rendering her oblivious to her surroundings.

The young deer was ending her life within the park, but she had been shot during the deer hunting season just beyond the park's western boundary, where she had lived. The bullet had not killed her, and she had fled in terror, eluding the hunter, who pursued but could not find her.

Coyote and her mate looked at each other. There were mouths to feed, and soon the heavier snows would come. As they approached the wounded deer, she whirled, attempting to flee, but fell to the ground in her weakened state, her legs thrashing in a vain effort to regain her footing. Coyote's mate—an agent this day of nature's compassion—descended on her neck with a powerful blow of his canines, swiftly ending her life and her suffering.

They must let their family know, and within moments Coyote howled for her pups, who immediately howled a response and ran toward their parents' call. Her mate had already opened the deer's abdomen, and the life-giving blood was flowing onto the white snow when the pups arrived. They had learned to delight in their wild food and ate hungrily beside their parents. Ravens croaked loudly in the fir above them, calling their yearling chicks to this table of plenty. As night fell, winged and furred carnivores would find their way to whatever was left. All were preparing for the approaching time of cold and hunger.

After they had eaten all they were able, Coyote and her mate broke through two of the deer's femur bones with their powerful jaws and canines, and each carried the flesh of her thighs back to the yearling. The pups trailed behind with bones they had licked clean held between their shiny white canines. They would all return to the carcass the next day, but with so many hungry mouths of the forest to feed, there might well be nothing left to eat by morning. Nothing would be wasted, not even the doe's blood, which sank into the frozen earth, offering the soil its rich nutrients for the coming spring.

When they lay the flesh of the deer before the yearling, she remained sitting while eating ravenously, for

141

in her weakness she was unable to stand for long. It had taken all her courage and reserves of strength to flee from the trap and keep moving onward. Now that she was safe, she had collapsed from the harrowing experience through which she had lived. Coyote's mate and young ones went off to rest as dusk drew near, but Coyote approached the yearling, licked the gaping wound of her mangled leg with her warm and healing tongue, and rested with her.

Weeks passed, and winter's bitter cold, blinding storms, and powerful winds arrived. The pups had reached their adult weight and become astute hunters under their parents' tutelage. The yearling female regained her strength, but the look in her eyes expressed the severe pain she experienced at all times. Her wounded leg was healing slowly with all the care from her new family. Over the next few months, the pain would lessen and her eyes would shine again.

A day came in which a peaceful morning of pale winter light gave way to an afternoon that was threatened by ominous, dark gray-blue clouds hovering over the mountains. In midafternoon, each member of the coyote family was hunting independently, seeking sustenance in a landscape blanketed by snow that was many feet deep in places. The storm began with a gentle dusting of flakes, then north winds arrived, gusting over the mountain peaks and bringing blizzard conditions. Squalls raced down the mountainsides and swirled through the valleys, creating whiteouts in churning whirlwinds of snow.

The smaller female pup, who had been hunting near the base of a steep mountain, struggled to find her way back to her parents through the blinding snow. She stopped and howled for her parents, who howled their response. She howled again, and again. Her parents again responded immediately to her frightened howls and moved toward her, leaping through high drifts and deep snow. Then, without warning, the mountain let go its heavy burden of snow in a powerful avalanche that crashed down on their small pup, covering her with twenty feet of snow and taking her life.

Her parents, scrambling as fast as they were able through the deep snow, heard the violent crashing of the avalanche and knew the cataclysm was taking place where their young one had been howling. Coyote's heart raced as she attempted to make her way even faster through the blinding snow, but she was already in mourning, for she knew her young one had been lost. She and her mate finally stopped, looked into each other's eyes, and howled, and howled again, and howled once more, hoping against hope that their young female would respond. But she did not. She was gone.

How was Coyote to grieve? How was she to endure the loss of this bright pup of hers who had been born so small but had survived and thrived and delighted in her young, happy life. She had been taken with no warning. Coyote could not save her; she could not respond fast enough to her pup's frightened howls through the deep and blinding snow. Standing where they had heard the pup's last howls, Coyote and her mate mournfully howled together. Silence. They fell onto the deep snow, the blizzard swirling around them, and remained in that spot and mourned together while the snow blanketed their sorrow.

That evening the blizzard ended, and the storm clouds were ushered east by softer westerly winds. All was still. No life moved under the deep blanket of white. Coyote and her mate slowly stood up, shaking off the thick blanket of snow that had covered their golden fur. Raising their faces to the evening sky, they howled their searching howl for their two young ones and their adopted yearling. Without delay, they heard two howls from the east and one from the south. They howled their searching howl once more, and, to their relief, the joyful howling of the young ones responded once more. The adults would travel through the forbidding winter landscape to reunite with the young.

But first, Coyote turned, her eyes searching the mountain, memorizing this spot. She stood silent while her mate came close and licked her muzzle. She would return in the spring to find her young one's body. She raised her head once more and uttered a haunting, mournful cry, then turned back and slowly struggled through the forbidding landscape with her mate by her side. There was no time to grieve now. They must help each other survive this winter.

Despite their unremitting parental teaching and solicitous care, they knew the first year of their pups' lives was one of constant peril. They had lost two of their four pups to deaths they could not prevent. Their young male with his golden coat had not even been four months old, and their little female had only been nine and a half months of age. As the two parents plowed through the deep snow to reunite with the young ones, they stopped from time to time to raise their mournful howl, and there was an understanding among all of the family that a great loss had been suffered. When the family reunited, licking muzzles and cuddling, the young ones knew they had lost their sister. A great sadness came over them as they curled up close to each other under a great fir in the silent, still landscape of white.

Their mournful cries did not go unnoticed. When the blizzard had begun, Peter, the ranger, and his wife, Caroline, had been camping near the coyotes' territory in the ranger's cabin, kept warm by a crackling woodstove. Caroline wanted to learn how coyotes survived the winter, for she was convinced that learning about their lives through the seasons was important. She wanted to help all the visitors to the park appreciate the value of this major carnivore to the landscape. She knew that before this park had been created in the 1930s, this forest, like so many others on the American continent, had

been devastated by clear-cutting, and all the large carnivores—wolves and cougars—had been persecuted and
wiped out. Now that this landscape had been protected,
it was slowly recovering and providing the habitat needed
for large, wide-ranging carnivores. Caroline was observing the return of a keystone predator to these forests—unnoticed, unknown, and unacknowledged by humans.

After reassuring her husband that she would not be
gone long, Caroline set out on the morning after the blizzard. She moved slowly through the deep snow with the
assistance of large snowshoes and ski poles that helped
her balance the pack she carried on her back. As she
traveled around a pond, she heard the mournful howls
of Coyote and her mate, again and again. She had heard
them howl on numerous occasions all summer and autumn, for she had taken every opportunity to venture
into what she thought was their territory in the park.
She had begun to recognize Coyote's howl and then her
mate's, and the pups' high-pitched excited yips were distinctive, but these howls were different. They were long
and low, and the mourning could not be mistaken. She
knew they had lost another pup in the blizzard. She
would keep her distance, giving them their space, for
they needed no other stress at this time.

Three days later, Caroline was trudging through deep
snow near a beaver dam when she began to see tracks,
coyote tracks. There were two of them, one following the
other in single file. She could tell that one was Coyote's

mate, for his stride was different due to his amputated paw and, if she looked deep into the snow, she could see that there was no paw mark on his back leg. She knew that their time to mate was coming soon, but this year they would have their surviving yearlings to help protect and hunt for the pups. She did not know about the young adopted female who had also become a part of their family.

While mulling these thoughts, she stopped short at the sight of blood strewn about on the snow and the minimal remains of what she suspected was a deer that had died of starvation. This was a time of death, for winter in the north woods is brutal and unforgiving and plays no favorites. She could tell that the whole family had been there, for there were numerous tracks about. She decided to take one of the bones that had been licked clean of flesh and left behind. The marrow would tell her if the deer had indeed died of starvation or perhaps been old or sick. She had traveled far enough for now, and it was time to return to the cabin. She wrapped the bone, stuffed it into her backpack, and headed back to the warmth of the wood-burning stove.

12

March to September 1972

The season that takes so many lives in the wild also brings forth the promise of new life to come. So it was for Coyote and her mate; it was their time. She was five years old, and her mate, four. She was an experienced mother now, and that experience made her even more careful, more alert, more solicitous.

Longer days and warmer sunshine embraced the landscape, and the snow cover yielded gradually to the earth's desire to be free of its winter coat. Ice began breaking up on streams and lakes, with large cracks echoing their grinding sounds over the valleys; huge chunks of ice vied with each other for the upper hand before shattering into ever smaller pieces. Coyote's pups were now almost a year old and thriving as skilled hunters while deepening their coyote sense. Coyote sense is a quality of wild intelligence, a wild sense of place on the landscape, a wild sense of relationship to family members and all life, a wild sense of self and purpose. But really there are no words for coyote sense.

Coyote sense was alive and well within the young adopted female, too; she was a survivor, just like Coyote's mate. Her leg was slowly healing, although it would often break open and bleed when she was trying too hard to keep up with the two young ones. She wanted to be a part of the family and to contribute to the hunting, for she knew that there would soon be newborn pups to protect and feed. She was excited to be an integral part of their upbringing. She was getting ready to be their aunt.

Two weeks before giving birth, Coyote sought out her mate, and together the two of them traveled to the base of the mountain where their little female had lost her life. She needed to find the pup and make real the tragedy of her death. Together they searched the landscape at the base of the mountain, their noses alert to the familiar smell of their pup. Then, after two hours of searching, she saw a paw stretching out from the snow. Coyote stopped and stared, then whimpered to her mate, who ran to her. Together, they brushed away the thick layer of snow covering her body. Their little female was lying with her front paws stretched out as though she had been attempting to free herself. Coyote was overcome with fresh grief, and her mournful howl traveled through the forest. They rested there for the rest of the afternoon, then carried her body under a great fir and covered her with wet needles that had fallen in the autumn. Now Coyote would know that this was her pup's resting place. She must leave now, for new life called to her.

All was hushed on the cool, crisp spring morning when Coyote's mate stood in anticipation at the entrance to the den. But he was not alone this time; three young ones stood beside him, excited, their ears cocked to the slightest sound of newborn whimpering. Then they heard! Silent anticipation was replaced by excited coyote dancing around the den mouth and yipping and yapping in happy celebration.

From within her den, Coyote heard her family's joy, but of the five pups to whom she had given birth, only four were alive. Her fifth tiny pup had been alive when born, but, within moments, had passed away. He was very little and weak, and the stress of his birth had been too much for him. She understood and accepted her loss, because she had to. Gently lifting his small, limp body in her mouth and placing him behind her, she embraced her four little pups, three females and one male, within her warm fur as they nursed for the first time.

The celebration went on outside the den. Coyote's family strained to hear any soft whimper from inside, then bounced back in their circling dance with each other, filling the air with excited yips and yaps.

Then the three young ones left to hunt while Coyote's mate remained, guarding the den. This year it need never be left unguarded, now that their family was becoming like that of their ancestors. They were on their way to returning to that ancient way of life. Before the young ones returned, Coyote emerged from the den with her small, lifeless pup and gave him to her mate. He licked her muzzle to comfort her in their loss but also to express his pleasure in their living new pups. As she stood at the den entrance, he walked over to a young spruce and tucked the pup's small body under its protecting branches. For a few moments they looked at each other, communicating in their silent language, and then she quietly slipped back into her den.

It was a bountiful spring and summer, for the two yearlings were excellent and accomplished hunters by now. They brought back to the den not only rodents of all kinds, but also rabbits, squirrels, trout, frogs, and a few times even a beaver. In early summer, for the first time in their lives, the two successfully chased down a newborn fawn under the experienced tutelage of their father. The four bouncing, happy pups had emerged from the den and were exploring their new world with their bright eyes and astute sense of smell, just as their older siblings had done a year before. On days when Coyote and her mate could take off together, the young adopted female loved to play with the little ones. She was most solicitous and on guard at all times but, at the same time, allowed the pups to climb all over her and tug at her tail.

The summer forest abounded with the throb of life, expressing itself in an array of burgeoning sounds—the awakening calls of songbirds in the morning twilight or their final territorial calls in the treetops at dusk, the croaking of frogs in ponds and wetlands, the snapping of branches and twigs on the forest floor as wild beings of all sizes and shapes moved through in their daily travels for survival, while above them gentle breezes created a soft flutter of leaves in the towering treetops. Friendly, warm skies sported a soft blue hue, and puffy clouds traveled through the sunshine on their way east, changing shape as they moved along.

By late summer, the four healthy pups were thriving, traveling farther and farther each day with their extended family looking after them. They explored every inch of their world, their little muzzles checking out the myriad smells on the forest floor or tucked within the forest's rocks and mosses, herbs and ferns. Everything was play; everything was fun; everything was a new adventure to be shared.

But then, two of the little female pups began vomiting their prey and experiencing bloody diarrhea. Their once happy, bouncing behavior changed drastically as grave weakness made it difficult for them to keep up with the family. Noticing the change immediately, their parents took turns resting with them while the others hunted. Soon the sick pups were refusing all food, nor would they drink. Coyote lay down with her little ones beside a small bubbling stream and held them close within her warm fur coat. There was nothing she could do to save them. She knew that, and her mate knew it too. One week later, her little pups passed away during the night, succumbing to the parvovirus. Through some miracle of nature, the other two pups were spared from this highly contagious disease.

As a wild mother, Coyote delighted in the perfect little lives she had brought into the world; but as a wild mother, she also paid the price of experiencing the death of her vulnerable little ones. Thus it is in the wild, and as a wild being, she understood that. But this did not diminish her grief. In the morning twilight, her mate looked into her eyes and understood that the little pups tucked within her fur had passed away.

As Coyote's family awoke, they all came to her. Her two yearlings, her adopted female, and her two remaining pups encircled her and, with quiet whining, sniffed the little ones who were gone. It was as though the forest mourned for the small pups as well, for the birds were not singing, and there was a silent stillness throughout. The family remained there together until late morning, when Coyote and her mate carried the departed pups to their resting place under a small, low-lying pine.

Coyote bore her grief deep within her wild soul, where it would dwell with the losses of last year's two pups. Knowing how to bear that grief with courage and dignity was part of who Coyote was. She would carry on, for her two pups and her yearlings needed her, and her mate needed her. After their evening hunting excursion, the family came together in their coyote circle, raised their muzzles to the starlit night, and sang their coyote song of family. Onward and upward their wild stirring song swirled into the night, bouncing off the mountainsides and treetops and echoing back. Their family was everything to them, and their song celebrated this before they settled down to rest for the night.

13

October 1972 to February 1975

Autumn in the north country followed swiftly after the luscious months of raspberries and blueberries. The change in the light and the migrations of birds were like alarms on the clock of time. Winter was on its way.

Coyote's yearling daughter, who had always been the dominant pup, began to travel to the far edges of their territory alone and stay away several days at a time. She was a year and a half old and testing her independence. She always returned, for she sensed that staying with her family was still the better choice. Their territory offered familiarity, an abundance of food, and the security of her family's presence. She was preparing herself for the day when she would leave for good, but that day was not yet.

The adopted young female, however, was ready. As winter locked the landscape, she was approaching her third birthday and taking long forays to the outer reaches of the family's territory. Each time she left, she stayed away longer and longer, testing her ability to survive alone. It had been more than a year now since she had escaped from the trap. Her mangled leg had healed, and she had adapted to the loss of her front paw, learning to hunt and catch prey in her own unique way. Her distinctive gait appeared sometimes more like hopping. It was that time of year when her female hormones, just like her adopted mother's, were awakening to the mating season. A restlessness took root in her, a growing desire to find a mate and create her own family. Coyote saw this and understood. They had helped her recover from the horrific experience of the trap and thrive as a member of the family. She had been an integral part of bringing up Coyote's second litter of pups. She was ready.

On a midwinter morning, she approached Coyote and her mate to bid farewell in the way only coyotes know. Saying goodbye is part of their lives. They understand. They licked each other's muzzles, stood looking at each other for a long time, and then she turned and headed southeast, the great mountain looming in all its majesty of ice and snow off to her right. She wandered along the southern edge of the park throughout the following spring and summer, howling at the night sky, yearning for a response but hearing none. But the many hikers that lay in their sleeping bags heard her song in wonder.

At times she traveled close to the southern boundary of Coyote's territory, and the family, recognizing her howls, would respond. In the autumn she traveled west, circling the great mountain and approaching another remote area that held one of the few remaining tracts of virgin forest in northeast America. One evening she once again raised her face to the sky and mournfully howled her song of longing. She had been alone since midwinter, and loneliness enveloped her. Just as she ended her song, an excited one responded. She sang again, and again heard an immediate response.

That night they found each other. He had been traveling from far to the west, alone so long in a world of traps, snares, dogs, and guns. But he had survived, and somehow he knew that he was safe here from human threats, though a coyote is never truly safe. But coyotes know their world as only coyotes can, and their survival is in that knowing.

As winter approached, Coyote was six and a half years old. She had become the matriarch of a growing family that now included two pups from her first litter, who were now two and a half years old; two surviving pups from her second litter, one female and one male, who were now one and a half; and the two surviving pups from this year, a female and a male. Her mate, the patriarch, was five and a half years old.

A coyote's family life is stable but dynamic and always changing, following a cycle of birth, learning, maturing, then dispersing, when young coyotes leave the family but somehow take it with them. The dominant female from Coyote's first litter had not been ready to leave the year before, but now she was ready. She knew it, and her mother knew it. After numerous forays outside her parents' territory, the time had come for her to leave for good.

The days were getting shorter, and the chill in the air was ever present, when she approached her mother and father, who were resting together in a sunny meadow near the great lake. The three of them nuzzled, cuddling with their heads over each other's necks in affection. The young female looked into her mother's eyes, and her mother into hers, and they bid farewell through the intimate bond of mother and daughter. There were no words, for coyotes need none to express their deep affection. With that, the young female turned and trotted away, looking over her shoulder at her parents until they were out of sight.

She traveled south, the same direction the young adopted female had initially taken the year before, and unknowingly placed herself in grave danger when she left the park in her wanderings. It was deer hunting season in Maine, and she heard guns in the forest, a terrifying sound that she had never heard within the park. Unfamiliar to her as well were the traps set along the park borders. Coyote and her mate had warned all their pups about the smell of humans and taught them to recognize that scent, which may be a sign of grave danger. Her mother had passed along the awareness that her own mother had taught her: *Beware of easy food that you have never learned to eat. Steer clear of it, for it is danger.* But her daughter's inexperience made her vulnerable to these potential threats outside the park.

Somehow her coyote sense and her parents' excellent tutelage protected her from guns and traps, for she changed the direction of her journey and unknowingly found her way back into the park again. Traveling around the southern base of the great mountain, she found numerous streams and large areas devoid of human trails. She settled in and made it her own territory, and by the following summer she met her mate, who had traveled south along the eastern side of the park. He too had somehow found his way past all the death traps and survived. His coyote savvy and strong character provided a perfect match for her own dominant personality. He was a formidable, imposing coyote, with long, handsome legs, an exquisite fur coat that made him look larger than life, and piercing golden eyes. They would bond with each other throughout the summer and autumn, and the following year they would have their own family of pups.

While her eldest daughter was finding her own territory and searching for a mate, Coyote and her mate welcomed their fourth litter of pups. Seven years old now, Coyote produced only two healthy pups, a female and a male. Again her extended family helped care for the pups and delighted in the little ones as if they were the first coyotes ever to be born. This would be her last litter, for next year she would be eight if she survived that long. She had become an excellent wild mother. These two little ones were the fortunate recipients of her vast experience.

She and her mate enjoyed a playful, happy summer with their family. Their surviving young ones of the past two years were healthy and strong, and their eldest son from the first litter had become a dominant member of the family, astute and wary, protective of all the younger ones. It was a good time in their lives. Cuddling in the evenings as crickets began their medley of summer music, Coyote and her mate, now the elders of the family, shared silent thoughts of the experiences of their lives. They had survived together, they had brought up their family together, and had seen their young ones begin to disperse and take their own journeys through life. They had delighted in this special place that was their home, where they had the freedom to be coyotes, to express their unique intelligence, to relate to their world in the way they saw fit.

As autumn drew to a close, Coyote could tell that her mate's coat did not look right. He was losing fur around his legs and haunches and relentlessly scratching himself in misery. She found him unable to settle down and sleep with her, and his ability to concentrate on his prey when hunting was greatly compromised. Soon he was unable to hunt at all, because the misery of the itching did not allow him to remain still and concentrate, and as a result, his prey always escaped. She recognized this affliction; one of her own siblings had died from it when only a tiny pup. The terrible condition was mange, caused by microscopic parasites that burrow under the skin. They multiply in the thousands, causing unbearable itching and almost constant scratching that will often lead to large open wounds. Adding to this misery is the progressive loss of fur due to the parasite's invasion of the follicles.

Coyote knew her mate's condition could lead to death, and she was determined to help him overcome it. She gathered her family to let them understand that they must all help hunt for their father, for he could not. The family united in their efforts to assist him in this dire time, hunting relentlessly despite the increasing snow cover and bitter cold. The situation was especially dire because he was losing fur just as the coldest nights of the season crept in. Bereft of his thick fur coat, he would soon freeze to death if not kept warm. Knowing this, she lay close to him, encircling his body with hers. She would do anything to save him, even risking the spread of the parasites to her own body. His blood from the open wounds stained the snow, and the light in his eyes grew dim, but he did not give up. His hearty coyote immune system fought to overcome the parasites in his body, and she gave him the courage to survive once more.

In the dead of winter, in bone-chilling cold and ever

deeper snow, their survival skills were stretched to their ultimate limit. Coyote would not leave him. She continued to keep him warm, and the family kept both of them well fed, for it was the time of year when old, weak, or crippled deer finally succumbed to winter's harsh ways. Again the ravens would alert the family, for they needed the coyotes to open the deer's body for them. Ravens and coyotes were a team in the struggle for survival.

As the days began to lengthen and the sun's warmth began to thaw the frozen landscape, Coyote noticed that her mate had stopped scratching and new fur was beginning to grow all over his body. He was recovering and wanting to hunt again, but he could not be apart from her long, as his fur coat had not yet recovered. She saw the glow come back into his eyes, and knew he had survived. Though the parasites had attempted to invade her body as well during this time, her strong immune system and support from their family had helped her halt the spread of the affliction. She was Coyote; she too would survive.

after numerous forays outside the family territory, and Coyote knew it was time. She feared for her daughter but must let her go. They romped and played together one last time, licked each other's muzzles, then her daughter turned and trotted away. She turned back repeatedly to look at her parents until she was out of sight, while Coyote and her mate stood together silently. They would never see her again.

But coyotes are never truly separated from one another; their bonds outlast farewells in a manner that is unknown outside their culture. This knowing remained with the daughter as she traveled west, skirting the southern slope of their raspberry mountain, respecting the territorial boundaries of her adopted sister, and followed the small mountain streams that led into the larger stream her parents had crossed when they discovered this special place. Traversing it where she could readily swim, she traveled farther west and out of the park. There she would survive against all odds and find her mate, who had dispersed from the Canadian interior like all the pioneering coyotes before him. And her daughter's daughters would continue to travel south and east, taking with them their coyote culture whose wavering spark had been nursed to an ember in the backcountry of the wild and beautiful protected forest of northern Maine.

Though keenly aware of the lack of new life in her family this year, Coyote knew that in territories just beyond hers, new life was being born. She recognized her daughters' voices and what they expressed when she heard them howling throughout the year. She knew her daughter and adopted daughter were mothers for the first time this year. And she knew they would be excellent mothers, for she had taught them herself, and they had learned by helping to take care of their younger siblings in the years before they had left. Her daughters would pass on the coyote culture she had received from her own mother. Their culture would not be lost.

In late autumn of that year, her eldest son was making the territorial rounds for his parents, leaving his scat in places to be noticed by all and spreading his scent on rocks and bushes. As he approached the turn of a brook that bordered the northern edge of the territory, something caught his attention. He raised his nose to an unfamiliar scent from across the brook. Back and forth, back and forth he trotted on the stream bank, reading and re-reading the scent. Dusk gathered, and he was on the verge of returning to his family when he heard a soft howling, then heard it again.

It was an unfamiliar voice, but it was a coyote voice and he knew it was speaking to him. He howled back softly and waited, and in the failing light he saw her face emerge from under a young white pine on the other side of the brook. She did not dare approach, for she understood well the coyote culture's exacting territorial deference. He crossed the brook and approached her slowly, sniffing the air; they looked into each other's eyes. How did these two wild beings communicate? What understandings passed from one to the other in wordless communication? How true and honest it must be; there are no doubts or misunderstandings, no concern over sincerity, only what is shared in a clear light.

Time seemed to stop as they stood facing each other. She spoke to him in silent sharing of her journey, and he understood. He was no longer a young coyote but his parents' eldest son, who had become a strong leader and proficient hunter. His parents had entrusted him with much responsibility for the survival and protection of their family. He welcomed her on his parents' behalf, and she stepped cautiously forward. He circled her as she lay on her back with her paws curled on her chest, exposing her abdomen in submission. There was such honesty in their encounter, and from that honesty came trust. He had learned this true communication from his parents, and she from hers. Coyote culture required this for their survival.

And then, as if on cue, she jumped up and shook out happily. He had accepted her. They cavorted and played as the stars of the night sky smiled on their joy. They must return to his family now, and indeed, just as he was about to guide her back, he heard his family's song calling him. He stopped momentarily, raised his nose to the full moon, and returned their song with his own. From his response, his parents knew right away that something special had happened, and they awaited him excitedly.

Coyote and her mate paced eagerly under a great fir, and the rest of their family felt their excitement and began to sing, wildly chasing every tone on the musical scale. At midnight they heard a crackling of branches and fallen leaves, and their son arrived. As he approached, he allowed the new female to come up alongside him. He moved directly toward his parents, speaking in wordless coyote communication. The young female again lay down on her back with her abdomen exposed and allowed Coyote and her mate to sniff all around her. Then each member of the family approached in turn, sniffed, and looked in her eyes.

The parents understood what their son intended; he wanted to welcome this young female as his future mate. Coyote welcomed her son's new mate with an exquisite song of joy under the full moon, and the whole family gathered around their new family member with noses lifted to the night sky, carrying on in a joyous song of welcome.

There were few campers in the park at this late time of year, but Caroline had made every effort to hike frequently into the remote area where Coyote and her mate lived. She wanted to understand all she could about them without intruding on their lives. Hearing their song that night as she lay snuggled in her sleeping bag at the campground, she noted an additional voice. She had been keeping copious records of the dispersals of the young females and the happenings in their territories as well, and she had seen that the ecosystem of the park was influenced by them in the most positive ways.

She observed the prey the coyote family survived on by inspecting their scat, and she recorded how their prey focus shifted with season. She noticed that ravens and small mammals were thriving, and black bears were doing well, too, for they would steal the coyotes' hard-won prey from time to time. She saw that young saplings were able to grow now instead of being immediately browsed unchecked by overabundant herbivores. She observed more butterflies, more wild flowers, more native bees. The coyotes were protecting these species' habitat from all-consuming herbivores of all sizes and shapes.

It was Caroline's intent to begin teaching those who came to the park about this new carnivore, the coyote. She wanted hikers to become more aware of the value of a climax predator's presence by observing positive changes in the park's ecosystem for themselves. What a rich experience it would be for hikers to truly observe what was happening, and not just pass through. She knew that someday soon, young coyotes would begin to disperse out of the protective shelter of the park. She hoped that informing citizens would in time ensure the protection of this important species not only in a park or preserve, but also across the landscape.

She wanted to be part of creating a new relationship with carnivores in this land, handing down a different world to future generations than the one that had been passed to hers. These remarkable wild beings of whom she had become so fond had unknowingly drawn her into their private world. The more she experienced of their lives, the more she wanted to experience. These coyotes had opened a new world to her, and she wanted to share it with others.

As winter commenced once more in the north country, descending with its blankets of snow and bitter cold, there came a singular excitement in the coyote family. In a manner only coyotes know, the eldest son expressed to his parents his desire to mate with the young female whom the whole family had welcomed in the autumn. It was her time, and she was in heat. Coyote herself would soon be nine years old, and her mate eight. They were now the elders, sharing their experience and knowledge and caring. It was time to pass on the bringing of new pups into the world to their son and his mate.

The parents shifted the roles they were to play, for their son would carry on when they were gone. Just as in the long-ago past, when coyotes had been free from persecution, their extended family would enrich their culture once more and begin handing it down from generation to generation. Though human settlers from Europe had never wished to share this land with wolves, cougars, or other predators, they had never been able to destroy the coyote culture. Coyotes carried it with them as they dispersed into new lands—and they will carry it into the future.

Coyote felt that she was nearing the end of her life.

Her body told her; she felt herself trotting more slowly now. Coyotes know death; it is part of their lives. Her mate, too, was showing his years in the silver-gray fur of his face. But they were joyful in the anticipation of the pups' birth and their son's new fatherhood.

And in early spring, that most momentous time in their lives came to pass, as they saw their son become the father of new pups and care for his mate as devotedly as his father had. It was especially important for the family to celebrate this event, for Coyote's two-year-old son, who had held so much promise as a future father and superb hunter, had fallen through the ice on the great lake and drowned just a month before the birth of the pups. Coyote and her mate had been mousing nearby when they heard his cries for help, but he was gone before they could reach the lake. All they had been able to do was witness the large crevice in the ice that had taken his life. Coyote had howled her deep grief as her mate stood close and joined his mournful cries. The rest of the family, hearing their parents, ran to them. A deep sense of sorrow ran through all as they circled around their parents, and then all lay down close together and remained there through the night.

There is much loss in a coyote's life, and for that reason, the birth of new life is a time of great celebration. The son's vibrant mate gave birth to six healthy little pups, and when they emerged from their den, the entire family was there to welcome and protect them, play with them, hunt for them, and celebrate them. It was a time of great comfort for Coyote and her mate, this one last experience of the arrival of new life.

It was a summer of fun and happiness for the whole family, for, in addition to their parents, the pups also enjoyed the care and playfulness of two aunts and two uncles—Coyote's maturing offspring—as well as Coyote and her mate's devoted attentiveness. Coyote's golden eyes glowed with pride and delight as she cuddled with her mate and saw the light in his eyes as well. The family's number had grown to fourteen with the birth of the pups, but that number would not remain. Despite all the care and attention showered on the little ones, living in the wild exposed them to danger in many guises, not all of which could be escaped.

In the early autumn, two of the little pups succumbed to parasites that devastated their internal organs and withered their small bodies. How many times in her life had Coyote mourned the death of little ones? Now her son and his mate and the whole family did as well. This was a coyote's life. Maybe that is why they sing to the night sky. Maybe their songs celebrate the short-lived joys of their lives, or maybe the songs share loss, lending comfort to the singers. Maybe coyotes sing for both reasons at once. And maybe they sing to celebrate the miracle of being here, inhabiting this moment, now, under this vast sky, astride this wild earth.

15

October 1976

One soft afternoon when birch leaves lit the mountainsides with gold once more, Coyote rested under a low-hanging spruce. She had carried her mother and father's genes through her long journey. She had carried their culture as well—coyote and wolf. She had found a remarkable mate who had been able to survive and thrive despite the suffering he had endured. She had found this very special refuge for her home and had brought four litters of pups into the world. Three of her grown pups had dispersed, two finding their own territories within the park and one venturing outside. She had endured the deaths of small pups but understood that their deaths were woven into the fabric of her life. She had delighted in the play that had brought so much joy to her mate and her young ones over the years, and she had sung her heart to the night sky. She had experienced the changes of the seasons and had breathed every new scent the

forest carried to her nose. She had been a huntress, seeking prey large and small with wit, not brawn, just as her
ancestors had done for millennia. She had left no waste
in the forest, but instead had enriched this place by her
presence. She had lived in freedom, accepting freedom's
harsh price.

Her eldest son and his mate had taken leadership of
the family and were thriving. Knowing that, Coyote was
at peace. She knew that her family would continue to
disperse from this protected place. In some recess of her
coyote consciousness she hoped there would be other
humans like Caroline—whom she had seen frequently
through the years—who would allow coyotes to be coyotes and respect their right to fulfill their purpose in life.

Then Coyote closed her eyes and left this world. A
soft breeze fluffed her golden fur as she lay still on a bed
of bright autumn leaves.

Two hours later, as evening drew down, Coyote's
mate called her but received no answer. Never had she
failed to respond to his call. Anxiously he sought her
out, following her scent through the forest, and he found
her at last, curled up as though peacefully sleeping. She
had not bid farewell to this mate to whom she was so
devoted. How could she say goodbye? Rather, she had
gone off by herself. He lay down next to her and did not
leave. Three days later, he joined her in death. There was
no living without her. They had lived their one precious
life to the fullest; they had delighted in the joys of their

life together and grieved deeply for their losses. They had brought new life into the world, and that new life would carry into the future.

The next morning the family found Coyote and her mate snuggled together. They had never known life without their parents. A hush came over the forest, almost an emptiness. Two vibrant beings who had trod the forest understory and swum the waters, who had sung to the night sky and slept under the great firs, who had run with glee together and chased prey at great speeds or pounced in surprise were gone now, but somehow they were not. It was as though they had joined their coyote ancestors to watch over those they had left behind. Feeling this, their family covered their bodies with light boughs and the richly colored leaves of oaks and maples, mixed with the scented needles of the spruce under which the bodies lay. That night the coyote family stood in a circle and, with faces lifted once more to the night sky, howled their profound grief and their farewell.

They remained beside their deceased parents throughout the night, but in the morning they left, for they needed to carry on.

16

August 1995 to the Present

Coyote had come to a new land wanting only to survive and live her one precious life to the fullest. Yet in nature's grand design she had accomplished much more: her presence on this landscape had begun to make it whole again, rich and diverse. She and her mate had pioneered the return of carnivores to the Maine woods. She had unknowingly led the way for others who would come behind her—the cougar and the wolf. She did not teach by words or any language humans know; she taught by who she was.

Her children carried on after her, dispersing from the protected confines of the park into places of great danger. But her descendants found other refuges in Maine and beyond, not parks or public lands but places where people lived and farmed. Though some people sought to persecute and kill them, many others wished to protect them and share the land with them. And Coyote's descendants would keep the next generations of humans in awe of their capacity to live alongside them quietly, unseen and unheard—until they sang their wild songs.

Coyote's vision played out once more on an early morning in central Maine, twenty years after her death. A female descendant, several generations later, stepped out of the forest into a farmer's field. It was a place rich in prey, for there were mice jumping around and numerous hares nibbling here and there. The farm was owned by a man named Ladislav, whose father had fled Czechoslovakia when Hitler invaded Prague and had bought a farm in Maine. The father had witnessed the violence that humans wreak when they call each other enemies, and he wanted to live in a place of peace, where no one was his enemy and there was no killing. The father had deeply instilled this way of living in Ladislav.

On the evening that she arrived at the farm, the young coyote raised her face to the stars and sang her song of yearning, her song reaching out into the meadows and the forests, as she searched for her own kind to answer. Her song found its way into the bedroom of the farmhouse where Ladislav and his wife, Rita, had just gone to bed. Hearing her song, they rushed to the open window and listened in wonder. That night they could hardly sleep, for they had experienced a profound wildness on their farm. In the morning, they spoke with each other at breakfast. "We should tell no one she is here," they said. "There will be no killing here."

Their farm was abundant with the animals Ladislav raised—sheep, goats, ducks, and chickens. His father had instilled in him the meaning of the Ancient Contract that humans had made when they had domesticated wild animals long ago. In exchange for milk, eggs, fiber, and flesh, farmers would provide the animals with food, water, shelter, and protection from dangers, including potential predation. On this farm, sturdy fences and protective housing had been erected, and the grazing animals were protected by two large guard dogs of a breed called Maremma, which had been guards in Italy for centuries. All of these husbandry practices spoke to carnivores in a language they understood—territorial boundaries and canine communication. When Ladislav and his wife heard Coyote's descendent singing, they knew she would understand, for their guard dogs spoke back to her. And she did understand. She continued to hunt the wild food her mother had taught her to seek.

Every evening into the autumn, the young coyote would sing her song, until one night she heard a response. Again she sang, and again she heard the response. The night was vibrant with wild music as the two young coyotes found each other and blended their ecstatic serenade. Ladislav and his wife raced to the window and gazed out, and in the light of the full moon they experienced a glimpse into the coyote's private world. Just inside the trees at the edge of the forest, the coyote pair could be glimpsed playing together, licking each other's muzzles, cavorting in joyful circles, then running off into the forest.

In the spring of the next year, the most joyful time of a coyote's life arrived with the birth of their pups. They needed to hunt more frequently now, so from time to time they would be out mousing or surprising hares during the day. It was then that they noticed the farmer gazing at them from afar, alerted by the barking of his guard dogs. He allowed them to be who they were. Later in the summer, Ladislav was thrilled to get a glimpse of the whole family, pups cavorting about and playing with their parents in the far meadow just at the edge of the forest. Before they all disappeared, he lifted his young son into his arms and began to teach him what his father had passed down to him. The coyote family came to know the farmer's heart, and he came to know theirs.

Coyote's vision of the future was coming true.

Author's Note

Coyote's journey ended with her death, but the journey of her descendants will continue into the future, for they have dispersed to all the lands in the east where wolves once roamed. As they strive to survive in a human-dominated world, they unknowingly do the work assigned to them by Nature, restoring balance, biodiversity, and protection from disease to the rest of life—and that includes us. Their journey is deeply interwoven with ours.

We have far to go to understand our profound relationship with coyotes, but the deeper that understanding becomes, the better we will understand ourselves as well. Maybe we don't know where we are going in our relationship with coyotes or how to get there, but the respect held by Native Peoples for this resilient carnivore might help us find our way.

We certainly know where we have been in the past and where we stand in the present. We know that coyotes, along with all other carnivores on the American continent, have been callously persecuted, and millions have lost their lives at the hands of humans who believe it is their God-given right to "control" them.

Today America's most resilient and successful carnivore, the coyote, has next to no protection in all 49 continental states. Anyone who wishes has the freedom to wantonly kill them. The Wildlife Services agency of the federal government, operating under the U.S. Department of Agriculture, guns down, traps, snares, and poisons coyotes by the tens of thousands every year, simply because they are coyotes, America's wild dog.

Each one of those tens of thousands is a sentient being, a wild soul, a distinct individual. Each one has been given by Nature a universal inheritance of inalienable rights—life, liberty, and the pursuit of happiness. These rights are not the heritage of the human species alone.

Where do we want to travel in our relationship with coyotes and with our wild planet, and how are we going to get there? I have attempted in this book to suggest a vision for the journey we might begin and our children might continue. May we shift our consciousness of other wild beings and grant ourselves the freedom to experience their lives from their point of view. A rich and marvelous future awaits our descendants if we seek a deeper understanding and compassion for these amazing wild ones. And all of Coyote's descendants will finally have the freedom to live in peace, as her vision foretold. Let our vision for the future be to allow wild beings to be who they are and thus enrich our lives.

Further Reading

The following books—arranged alphabetically by title—are recommended to anyone who is inspired to read more about the ecology of coyotes and their relationship to our human species.

Books for All Ages

Changes in the Land, rev. ed., William Cronon (Hill and Wang, 2003)
This well-researched account describes how Native Americans and early European colonists used the land and related to the wildlife of northeastern America, and how the complex natural system broke down as a result of the European occupation of America.

The Conquest of Paradise: Christopher Columbus and the Columbian Legacy, Kirkpatrick Sale (Knopf, 1990)
Sale describes in detail how Europeans treated the land and wildlife of Europe, then takes us on the journeys of Christopher Columbus and describes the consequences for life on the American continent.

Coyote: Defiant Song Dog of the West, rev. ed., Francois Leydet (Chronicle, 1988)
A thoroughly researched, deeply moving account of coyotes' struggle for survival and their relationship with humans, past and present, revealing much about ourselves and our interactions with wild carnivores.

Don Coyote: The Good Times and the Bad Times of a Much Maligned American Original, **Dayton Hyde** (Arbor House, 1986)
Hyde is an Oregon rancher who understands that his ranch is an ecosystem. This is his personal story of respect for the land and the wild beings he shares it with, especially coyotes.

The Eastern Coyote: The Story of Its Success, **Gerry Parker** (Nimbus, 1995)
A good source for coyote biology and behavior. Parker is a biologist in New Brunswick, Canada, who has conducted much research on coyotes. Be sure to read the poem he wrote at the end of the book.

God's Dog, **Hope Ryden** (Lyons and Burford, 1979)
This book, the result of the author's many years of observing coyote behavior in the wild, provides a thorough understanding of coyotes' complex social life and ecology and their intimate relationships with one another.

Moon Song, **Byrd Baylor** (Scribner, 1982)
A testimony of respect and honor for our native wild dog, the coyote, in prose that approaches poetry.

Predatory Bureaucracy: The Extermination of the Wolves and the Transformation of the West, **Michael Robinson** (University Press of Colorado, 2005)
A thorough historical perspective of predator control as it evolved in this country and is practiced today. It is important to learn about the atrocities heaped on our native carnivores, and with that perspective to seek solutions for coexistence for the future.

The Voice of the Coyote, **Second Edition, Frank Dobie** (Bison Books, 2006)

A classic! This is an outstanding introduction to coyotes with a historical perspective. The first book I would recommend to any American who is interested in coyotes.

Where the Wild Things Were: Life, Death and Ecological Wreckage in a Land of Vanishing Predators, **William Stolzenburg** (Bloomsbury USA, 2009)

Relates the research experiences of leading conservation biologists and ecologists who have investigated carnivores and how they dramatically affect ecosystems. Wonderful storytelling makes this a book you will not want to put down.

Books for Young Readers

At the Edge of the Forest, **Jonathan London** (Candlewick, 1998)

A little boy teaches his father to respect the needs of wild parents while at the same time protecting his farm animals from predation. The author thoughtfully expresses the wisdom of the child, who understands our human place in the world.

Coyote: The Barking Dog, **Natalie Lunis** (Bearport, 2011)

With great photos and succinct information presented in an inviting and straightforward way, Lunis shares with children who this amazing carnivore really is.

Two Coyotes*, *Carol Carrick (Houghton Mifflin, 1982)
This wonderful, beautifully illustrated book explores the difficult lives of coyotes who live in the north. It reveals the role of the predator-prey relationship in the life and survival of wild carnivores, a subject that is too rarely expressed in children's books but so important for children to experience. It also describes the intimate lives of coyote mates and their support of each other in the battle for survival.

To hear Coyote's song, scan the QR code below. It is impossible to hear it and not know that other sentient beings share this planet with us. Ours is not the only consciousness that kindles sparks in the darkness.

http://www.tilburyhouse.com/bookstore/i-am-coyote/

Geri Vistein is a carnivore conservation biologist who holds a masters degree in wildlife conservation and a masters in education. From early participation in studies of predator-prey relationships, including a grizzly bear DNA study in and around Glacier National Park, an elk calf mortality study on ranches in the Black-foot Valley, and a snowshoe hare study in Yellowstone National Park, her professional mission evolved to a focus on helping human communities understand and coexist with carnivores. Now a resident of Maine, she concentrates her work on coyotes, speaking extensively about coyote-human interactions and maintaining an educational website at www.CoyoteLivesinMaine.com.